Relational and XML Data Exchange

Relational and XML Data Exchange

Marcelo Arenas, Pablo Barceló, Leonid Libkin, and Filip Murlak

ISBN: 978-3-031-00712-5   paperback
ISBN: 978-3-031-01840-4   ebook

DOI 10.1007/978-3-031-01840-4

A Publication in the Springer series
SYNTHESIS LECTURES ON DATA MANAGEMENT

Lecture #8
Series Editor: M. Tamer Özsu, *University of Waterloo*
Series ISSN
Synthesis Lectures on Data Management
Print 2153-5418   Electronic 2153-5426

Synthesis Lectures on Data Management

Editor
M. Tamer Özsu, *University of Waterloo*

Synthesis Lectures on Data Management is edited by Tamer Özsu of the University of Waterloo. The series will publish 50- to 125 page publications on topics pertaining to data management. The scope will largely follow the purview of premier information and computer science conferences, such as ACM SIGMOD, VLDB, ICDE, PODS, ICDT, and ACM KDD. Potential topics include, but not are limited to: query languages, database system architectures, transaction management, data warehousing, XML and databases, data stream systems, wide scale data distribution, multimedia data management, data mining, and related subjects.

Relational and XML Data Exchange
Marcelo Arenas, Pablo Barceló, Leonid Libkin, and Filip Murlak
2010

Database Replication
Bettina Kemme, Ricardo Jiménez Peris, and Marta Patiño-Martínez
2010

User-Centered Data Management
Tiziana Catarci, Alan Dix, Stephen Kimani, and Giuseppe Santucci
2010

Data Stream Management
Lukasz Golab and M. Tamer Özsu
2010

Access Control in Data Management Systems
Elena Ferrari
2010

An Introduction to Duplicate Detection
Felix Naumann and Melanie Herschel
2010

Privacy-Preserving Data Publishing: An Overview
Raymond Chi-Wing Wong and Ada Wai-Chee Fu
2010

Keyword Search in Databases
Jeffrey Xu Yu, Lu Qin, and Lijun Chang
2009

Relational and XML Data Exchange

Marcelo Arenas
Pontificia Universidad Católica de Chile

Pablo Barceló
University of Chile

Leonid Libkin
University of Edinburgh

Filip Murlak
University of Warsaw

SYNTHESIS LECTURES ON DATA MANAGEMENT #8

ABSTRACT

Data exchange is the problem of finding an instance of a target schema, given an instance of a source schema and a specification of the relationship between the source and the target. Such a target instance should correctly represent information from the source instance under the constraints imposed by the target schema, and it should allow one to evaluate queries on the target instance in a way that is semantically consistent with the source data. Data exchange is an old problem that re-emerged as an active research topic recently, due to the increased need for exchange of data in various formats, often in e-business applications.

In this lecture, we give an overview of the basic concepts of data exchange in both relational and XML contexts. We give examples of data exchange problems, and we introduce the main tasks that need to addressed. We then discuss relational data exchange, concentrating on issues such as relational schema mappings, materializing target instances (including canonical solutions and cores), query answering, and query rewriting. After that, we discuss metadata management, i.e., handling schema mappings themselves. We pay particular attention to operations on schema mappings, such as composition and inverse. Finally, we describe both data exchange and metadata management in the context of XML. We use mappings based on transforming tree patterns, and we show that they lead to a host of new problems that did not arise in the relational case, but they need to be addressed for XML. These include consistency issues for mappings and schemas, as well as imposing tighter restrictions on mappings and queries to achieve tractable query answering in data exchange.

KEYWORDS

data exchange, schema mappings, dependencies, chase, universal solutions, conjunctive queries, query rewriting, mapping composition, mapping inverse, XML patterns, mapping consistency, XML data exchange

Contents

CHAPTER 1

Overview

Data exchange is the problem of finding an instance of a target schema, given an instance of a source schema and a specification of the relationship between the source and the target. Such a target instance should correctly represent information from the source instance under the constraints imposed by the target schema, and it should allow one to evaluate queries on the target instance in a way that is semantically consistent with the source data.

Data exchange is an old problem that re-emerged as an active research topic recently due to the increased need for exchange of data in various formats, often in e-business applications.

The general setting of data exchange is this:

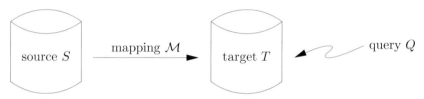

We have fixed source and target schemas, an instance S of the source schema, and a mapping $\mathcal{M}$ that specifies the relationship between the source and the target schemas. The goal is to construct an instance T of the target schema, based on the source and the mapping, and answer queries against the target data in a way consistent with the source data.

The goal of this introductory chapter is to make precise some of the key notions of data exchange: schema mappings, solutions, source-to-target dependencies, certain answers. We do it by means of an example we present in the next section.

1.1   A DATA EXCHANGE EXAMPLE

Suppose we want to create a database containing three relations:

- ROUTES(flight#,source,destination)

  This relation has information about routes served by several airlines: it has a flight# attribute (e.g., AF406 or KLM1276), as well as source and destination attributes (e.g., Paris and Santiago for AF406).

- INFO_FLIGHT(flight#,departure_time,arrival_time,airline)

  This relation provides additional information about the flight: departure and arrival times, as well as the name of an airline.

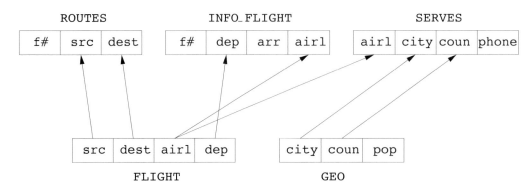

Figure 1.1: Schema mapping: a simple graphical representation

• SERVES(airline,city,country,phone)

This relation has information about cities served by airlines: for example, it may have a tuple (AirFrance, Santiago, Chile, 5550000), indicating that Air France serves Santiago, Chile, and its office there can be reached at 555-0000.

We do not start from scratch: there is a source database available from which we can transfer information. This source database has two relations:

• FLIGHT(source,destination,airline,departure)

This relation contains information about flights, although not all the information needed in the target. We only have source, destination, and airline (but no flight number), and departure time (but no arrival time).

• GEO(city,country,population)

This relation has some basic geographical information: cities, countries where they are located, and their population.

As the first step of moving the data from the source database into our target, we have to specify a *schema mapping*, a set of relationships between the two schemas. We can start with a simple graphical representation of such a mapping shown in Figure 1.1. The arrows in such a graphical representation show the relationship between attributes in different schemas.

But simple connections between attributes are not enough. For example, when we create records in ROUTES and INFO_FLIGHT based on a record in FLIGHT, we need to ensure that the values of flight# attribute (abbreviated as f# in the Figure) are the same. This is indicated by a curved line connecting these attributes. Likewise, when we populate table SERVES, we only want to include cities which appear in table FLIGHT – this is indicated by the line connecting attributes in tables GEO and FLIGHT.

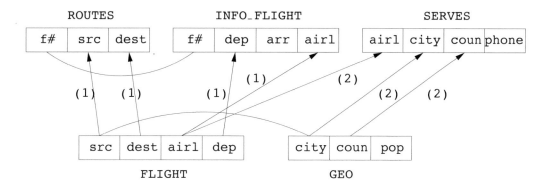

Figure 1.2: Schema mapping: a proper graphical representation

Furthermore, there are several *rules* in a mapping that help us populate the target database. In this example, we can distinguish two rules. One uses table FLIGHT to populate ROUTES and INFO_FLIGHT, and the other uses both FLIGHT and GEO to populate SERVES. So, in addition, we annotate arrows with names or numbers of rules that they are used in. Such a revised representation is shown in Figure 1.2.

While it might be easy for someone understanding source and target schemas to produce a graphical representation of the mapping, we need to translate it into a formal specification. Let us look at the first rule which says:

> *whenever we have a tuple* (src,dest,airl,dep) *in relation* FLIGHT, *we must have a tuple in* ROUTES *that has* src *and* dest *as the values of the second and the third attributes, and a tuple in* INFO_FLIGHT *that has* dep *and* airl *as the second and the fourth attributes.*

Formally, this can be written as:

$$\text{FLIGHT(src,dest,airl,dep)} \longrightarrow$$
$$\text{ROUTES(\_,src,dest), INFO\_FLIGHT(\_,dep,\_,airl)}$$

This is not fully satisfactory: indeed, as we lose information that the flight numbers must be the same; we need to explicitly mention names of all the variables and produce the following rule:

$$\text{FLIGHT(src,dest,airl,dep)} \longrightarrow$$
$$\text{ROUTES(f\#,src,dest), INFO\_FLIGHT(f\#,dep,arr,airl)}$$

What is the meaning of such a rule? In particular, what are those variables that appear in the target specification without being mentioned in the source part? What the mapping says is that values for these variables must *exist* in the target, in other words, the following must be satisfied:

$$\text{FLIGHT(src,dest,airl,dep)} \longrightarrow$$
$$\exists\text{f\#}\, \exists\text{arr}\, \big(\, \text{ROUTES(f\#,src,dest)} \wedge \text{INFO\_FLIGHT(f\#,dep,arr,airl)} \,\big)$$

To complete the description of the rule, we need to clarify the role of variables `src`, `dest`, `airl` and `dep`. The meaning of the rule is that *for every* tuple (`src`,`dest`,`airl`,`dep`) in table FLIGHT, we have to create tuples in relations ROUTES and INFO_FLIGHT of the target schema. Hence, finally, the meaning of the first rule is:

$$\forall \mathtt{src}\ \forall \mathtt{dest}\ \forall \mathtt{airl}\ \forall \mathtt{dep}\ \Big(\ \mathtt{FLIGHT(src,dest,airl,dep)} \longrightarrow$$
$$\exists \mathtt{f\#}\ \exists \mathtt{arr}\ \big(\ \mathtt{ROUTES(f\#,src,dest)} \wedge \mathtt{INFO\_FLIGHT(f\#,dep,arr,airl)}\ \big)\Big)$$

Note that this is a query written in relational calculus, without free variables. In other words, it is a sentence of first-order logic, over the vocabulary including both source and target relations. The meaning of this sentence is as follows: given a source S, a target instance we construct is such that together, S and T satisfy this sentence.

We now move to the second rule. Unlike the first, it looks at two tuples in the source: (`src`,`dest`,`airl`,`dep`) in FLIGHT and (`city`,`country`,`popul`) in GEO. If they satisfy the join condition `city=scr`, then a tuple needs to be inserted in the target relation SERVES:

$$\mathtt{FLIGHT(src,dest,airl,dep)}, \mathtt{GEO(city,country,popul)}, \mathtt{city=src} \longrightarrow$$
$$\mathtt{SERVES(airl,city,country,phone)}$$

As with the first rule, the actual meaning of this rule is obtained by explicitly quantifying the variables involved:

$$\forall \mathtt{city}\ \forall \mathtt{dest}\ \forall \mathtt{airl}\ \forall \mathtt{dep}\ \forall \mathtt{country}\ \forall \mathtt{popul}\ \Big($$
$$\mathtt{FLIGHT(city,dest,airl,dep)} \wedge \mathtt{GEO(city,country,popul)} \longrightarrow$$
$$\exists \mathtt{phone}\ \mathtt{SERVES(airl,city,country,phone)}\ \Big)$$

We can also have a similar rule in which the destination city is moved in the SERVES table in the target:

$$\forall \mathtt{city}\ \forall \mathtt{dest}\ \forall \mathtt{airl}\ \forall \mathtt{dep}\ \forall \mathtt{country}\ \forall \mathtt{popul}\ \Big($$
$$\mathtt{FLIGHT(src,city,airl,dep)} \wedge \mathtt{GEO(city,country,popul)} \longrightarrow$$
$$\exists \mathtt{phone}\ \mathtt{SERVES(airl,city,country,phone)}\ \Big)$$

These rules together form what we call a *schema mapping*: a collection of rules that specify the relationship between the source and the target. When we write them, we actually often omit universal quantifiers $\forall$, as they can be reconstructed by the following rule:

- every variable mentioned with one of the source relations is quantified universally.

With these conventions, we arrive at the following schema mapping $\mathcal{M}$:

```
(1)  FLIGHT(src,dest,airl,dep) ⟶
        ∃f# ∃arr (ROUTES(f#,src,dest) ∧ INFO_FLIGHT(f#,dep,arr,airl))

(2)  FLIGHT(city,dest,airl,dep) ∧ GEO(city,country,popul) ⟶
        ∃phone SERVES(airl,city,country,phone)

(3)  FLIGHT(src,city,airl,dep) ∧ GEO(city,country,popul) ⟶
        ∃phone SERVES(airl,city,country,phone)
```

Now, what does it mean to have a target instance, given a source instance and a mapping? Since mappings are logical sentences, we want target instances to satisfy these sentences, with respect to the source. More precisely, note that mappings viewed as logical sentences mention both source and target schemas. So possible target instances T for a given source S must satisfy the following condition:

For each condition φ of the mapping $\mathcal{M}$, the pair (S, T) satisfies φ.

We call such instances T *solutions for S under* $\mathcal{M}$. Look, for example, at our mapping $\mathcal{M}$, and assume that the source S has a tuple (*Paris, Santiago, AirFrance*, 2320). Then every solution T for S under $\mathcal{M}$ must have tuples

$(x, Paris, Santiago)$ in ROUTES and $(x, 2320, y, AirFrance)$ in INFO_FLIGHT

for some values x and y, interpreted as flight number and arrival time. The mapping says nothing about these values: they may be real values (constants), e.g., (406, *Paris, Santiago*), or *nulls*, indicating that we lack this information at present. We shall normally use the symbol $\bot$ to denote nulls, so a common way to populate the target would be with tuples ($\bot$, *Paris, Santiago*) and ($\bot$, 2320, $\bot'$, *AirFrance*). Note that the first attributes of both tuples, while being unknown, are nonetheless the same. This situation is referred to as having *marked nulls*, or *naïve* nulls, as they are used in naïve tables, studied extensively in connection with incomplete information in relational databases. At the same time, we know nothing about the other null $\bot'$ used: nothing prevents it from being different from $\bot$ but nothing tells us that it should be.

Note that already this simple example leads to a crucial observation that makes the data exchange problem interesting: *solutions are not unique*. In fact, there could be infinitely many solutions: we can use different marked nulls, or we can instantiate them with different values.

If solutions are not unique, how can we answer queries? Consider, for example, a Boolean (yes/no) query *"Is there a flight from Paris to Santiago that arrives before 10am?"* The answer to this query has to be 'no' even though in some solutions we shall have tuples with arrival time before 10am. However, in others, in particular in the one with null values, the comparison with 10am will not evaluate to true, and thus we have to return 'no' as the answer.

On the other hand, the answer query *"Is there a flight from Paris to Santiago?"* is 'yes', as the tuple including Paris and Santiago will be in every solution. Intuitively, what we want to do in query answering in data exchange is to return answers that will be true in every solution. These are called *certain answers*; we shall define them formally shortly.

1.1.1   XML DATA EXCHANGE

Before outlining the key tasks in data exchange, we briefly look at the XML representation of the above problem. XML is a flexible data format for storing and exchanging data on the Web. XML documents are essentially trees, that can represent data organized in a way more complex than the usual relational databases. But each relational database can be encoded as an XML document; a portion of our example database, representing information about the Paris–Santiago flight and information about Santiago, is shown in the picture below.

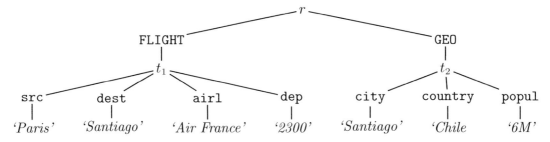

The tree has a root r with two children, corresponding to relations FLIGHT and GEO. Each of those has several children, labeled t_1 and t_2, respectively, corresponding to tuples in the relations. We show one tuple in each relation in the example. Each t_1-node has four children that correspond to the attributes of FLIGHT and each t_2-node has three children, with attributes of GEO. Finally, each of the attribute nodes has a child holding the value of the attribute.

To reformulate a rule in a schema mapping in this language, we show how portions of trees are restructured. Consider, for example, the rule

$$\text{FLIGHT(city,dest,airl,dep)} \wedge \text{GEO(city,country,popul)} \longrightarrow$$
$$\exists\text{phone SERVES(airl,city,country,phone)}$$

We restate it in the XML context as follows:

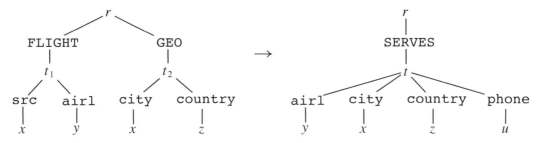

That is, if we have tuples in FLIGHT and GEO that agree on the values of the source and city attributes, we grab the values of the airline and country attributes, invent a new value u for phone and create a tuple in relation SERVES.

The rules of XML schema mappings are thus represented via *tree patterns*. Essentially, they say that if a certain pattern occurs in a source document, some other pattern, obtained by its restructuring, must occur in the target.

This view of XML schema mappings is not surprising if we note that in our relational examples, the rules are obtained by using a relational pattern – i.e., a conjunction of source atoms – and rearranging them as a conjunction of target atoms. Conjunctions of atoms are natural analogs of tree patterns. Indeed, the pattern on the right-hand side of the above rule, for example, can be viewed as the conjunction of the statements about existence of the following edge relations: between the root and a node labeled SERVES, between that node an a node labeled t, between the t-node and nodes labeled airl, city, country, and phone, respectively, and between those nodes and nodes carrying attribute values y, x, z, and u.

Of course, we shall see when we describe XML data exchange that patterns could be significantly more complicated: they need not be simple translations of relational atoms. In fact, one can use more complicated forms of navigation such as the horizontal ordering of siblings in a document, or the descendant relation. But for now, our goal was to introduce the idea of tree patterns by means of a straightforward translation of a relational example.

1.2   OVERVIEW OF THE MAIN TASKS IN DATA EXCHANGE

The key tasks in many database applications can be roughly split into two groups:

1. *Static analysis.* This mostly involves dealing with schemas; for example, the classical relational database problems such as dependency implication and normalization fall into this category. Typically, the input one considers is (relatively) small, e.g., a schema, a set of constraints. Therefore, somewhat higher complexity bounds are normally tolerated: for example, many problems related to reasoning about dependencies are complete for complexity classes such as NP, or coNP, or PSPACE.

2. *Dealing with data.* These are the key problems such as querying or updating the data. Of course, given that databases are typically large, only low-complexity algorithms are tolerated when one handles data. For example, the complexity of evaluating a fixed relational algebra query is very low (AC^0, to be precise), and even more expressive languages such as Datalog stay in PTIME.

In data exchange, the key tasks too can be split into two groups. For static analysis tasks, we treat schema mappings as first-class citizens. The questions one deals with are generally of two kinds:

• *Consistency.* For these questions, the input is a schema mapping $\mathcal{M}$, and the question is whether it makes sense: for example, whether there exists a source S that has a solution under $\mathcal{M}$, or whether all sources of a given schema have solutions. These analysis are important for ruling out "bad" mappings that are unlikely to be useful in data exchange.

- *Operations on mappings.* Suppose we have a mapping $\mathcal{M}$ from a source schema $\mathbf{R_s}$ to a target schema $\mathbf{R_t}$, and another mapping $\mathcal{M}'$ that uses $\mathbf{R_t}$ as the source schema and maps it into a schema $\mathbf{R_u}$. Can we combine these mappings into one, the composition of the two, $\mathcal{M} \circ \mathcal{M}'$, which maps $\mathbf{R_s}$ to $\mathbf{R_u}$? Or can we invert a mapping, and find a mapping $\mathcal{M}^{-1}$ from $\mathbf{R_t}$ into $\mathbf{R_s}$, that undoes the transformation performed by $\mathcal{M}$ and recovers as much original information about the source as possible? These questions arise when one considers schema evolution: as schemas evolve, so do the mappings between them. And once we understand when and how we can construct mappings such as $\mathcal{M} \circ \mathcal{M}'$ or $\mathcal{M}^{-1}$, we need to understand their properties with respect to the 'existence of solutions' problem.

Tasks involving data are generally of two kinds.

- *Materializing target instances.* Suppose we have a schema mapping $\mathcal{M}$ and a source instance S. Which target instance do we materialize? As we already saw, there could be many – perhaps infinitely many – target instances which are solutions for S under $\mathcal{M}$. Choosing one, we should think of three criteria:

  1. it should faithfully represent the information from the source, under the constraints imposed by the mapping;

  2. it should not contain (too much) redundant information;

  3. the computational cost of constructing the solution should be reasonable.

- *Query answering.* Ultimately, we want to answer queries against the target schema. As we explained, due the existence of multiple solutions, we need to answer them in a way that is consistent with the source data. So if we have a materialized target T and a query Q, we need to find a way of evaluating it to produce the set of certain answers. As we shall see, sometimes computing $Q(T)$ does *not* give us certain answers, so we may need to change Q into another query Q' and then evaluate Q' on a chosen solution to get the desired answer. The complexity of this task will also depend on a class of queries to which Q belongs. We shall see that for some classes, constructing Q' is easy, while for others, Q' must come from languages much more expressive (and harder to evaluate) than SQL, and for some, it may not even exist.

1.3   KEY DEFINITIONS

We now get a bit more formal and present the key definitions related to data exchange. For a relational schema $\mathbf{R}$, we let $\text{INST}(\mathbf{R})$ stand for the set of all database instances of $\mathbf{R}$. We start with

- a *source schema* $\mathbf{R_s}$,

- a *target schema* $\mathbf{R_t}$, and

- a set Σ_{st} of *source-to-target dependencies.*

Source-to-target dependencies, or *stds*, are logical sentences over $\mathbf{R_s}$ and $\mathbf{R_t}$; for example,

$$\forall \text{src } \forall \text{dest } \forall \text{airl } \forall \text{dep} \Big(\text{FLIGHT(src,dest,airl,dep)} \longrightarrow$$
$$\exists \text{f\# } \exists \text{arr} \big(\text{ROUTES(f\#,src,dest)} \wedge \text{INFO\_FLIGHT(f\#,dep,arr,airl)} \big) \Big)$$

We may also have

- a set of target dependencies Σ_t, i.e., logical sentences over $\mathbf{R_t}$. These are typical database integrity constraints such as keys and foreign keys.

We define a *schema mapping* as a quadruple

$$\mathcal{M} = (\mathbf{R_s}, \mathbf{R_t}, \Sigma_{st}, \Sigma_t),$$

or just $(\mathbf{R_s}, \mathbf{R_t}, \Sigma_{st})$, when there are no target constraints.

Now assume S is a *source instance*, i.e., a database instance over $\mathbf{R_s}$. Then a target instance T is called a *solution for S under $\mathcal{M}$* if and only if S and T together satisfy all the stds in Σ_{st}, and T satisfies all the constraints in Σ_t. That is, T is a solution for S under $\mathcal{M}$ if

$$(S, T) \models \Sigma_{st} \text{ and } T \models \Sigma_t.$$

For mappings without target constraints, we only require $(S, T) \models \Sigma_{st}$. The set of all solutions for S under $\mathcal{M}$ is denoted by $\text{SOL}_{\mathcal{M}}(S)$:

$$\text{SOL}_{\mathcal{M}}(S) = \{T \in \text{INST}(\mathbf{R_t}) \mid (S, T) \models \Sigma_{st} \text{ and } T \models \Sigma_t\}.$$

Semantically, we can view the mapping $\mathcal{M}$ as a binary relation between $\text{INST}(\mathbf{R_s})$ and $\text{INST}(\mathbf{R_t})$, i.e., $[\![\mathcal{M}]\!] \subseteq \text{INST}(\mathbf{R_s}) \times \text{INST}(\mathbf{R_t})$ is defined as

$$[\![\mathcal{M}]\!] = \{(S, T) \mid S \in \text{INST}(\mathbf{R_s}), \ T \in \text{INST}(\mathbf{R_t}), \text{ and } T \in \text{SOL}_{\mathcal{M}}(S)\}.$$

If we have a query Q over the target schema $\mathbf{R_t}$, we want to compute *certain answers*; these are answers true in all solutions for a given source instance S. That is, certain answers are defined as

$$certain_{\mathcal{M}}(Q, S) = \bigcap_{T \in \text{SOL}_{\mathcal{M}}(S)} Q(T).$$

We want to compute $certain_{\mathcal{M}}(Q, S)$ using just one specific materialized solution, say T_0. In general, $Q(T_0)$ need not be equal $certain_{\mathcal{M}}(Q, S)$. Instead, one is looking for a different query Q', called a *rewriting of Q*, so that

$$Q'(T_0) = certain_{\mathcal{M}}(Q, S).$$

When we have such a materialized solution T_0 and a rewriting Q' for each query Q we want to pose, we have the answer to the two key questions of data exchange. First, we know which solution to materialize – it is T_0. Second, we know how to answer queries – compute the rewriting Q' of Q and apply it to T_0.

1.4   BACKGROUND

We assume that the reader is familiar with the following.

Relational database model We expect the reader to have seen the relational database model and be familiar with the standard notions of schemas, instances, constraints, and query languages. In particular, we assume the knowledge of the following:

- Basic relational query languages, especially relational calculus (i.e., first-order predicate logic, often abbreviated as FO) and its fragments such as:

  1. Conjunctive queries, also known as select-project-join queries, formally defined as the $\exists, \wedge$-fragment of FO, or the $\sigma, \pi, \times$-fragment of relational algebra; and
  2. Unions of conjunctive queries, that correspond to select-project-join-union queries.

- Relational integrity constraints, especially keys and foreign keys, and more generally, functional and inclusion dependencies.

XML Although we define the key XML concepts we need, it would help the reader to have seen them before. We assume the basic knowledge of automata on words (strings); all the concepts related to automata on trees will be defined here.

1.5   BIBLIOGRAPHIC COMMENTS

Data exchange, also known as data translation, is a very old problem that arises in many tasks where data must be transferred between independent applications [Housel et al., 1977]. Examples of data exchange problems appeared in the literature over 30 years ago. But as the need for data exchange increased over the years [Bernstein, 2003], research prototypes appeared [Fagin et al., 2009] and made their way into commercial database products. The theory was lagging behind until the paper by Fagin et al. [2005a] which presented the widely accepted theoretical model of data exchange. It developed the basis of the theory of data exchange, by identifying the key problems and looking into materializing target instances and answering queries.

Within a year or two of the publication of the conference version of this paper, data exchange grew into a dominant subject in the database theory literature, with many papers published in conferences such as PODS, SIGMOD, VLDB, ICDT, etc. By now, there are several papers presenting surveys of various aspects of relational data exchange and schema mappings [Barceló, 2009; Bernstein and Melnik, 2007; Kolaitis, 2005]; extensions to XML have been described as well [Amano et al., 2009; Arenas and Libkin, 2008]. Much more extensive bibliographic comments will be provided in the subsequent chapters.

The subject of data integration has also received much attention, see, for example, Haas [2007] and Lenzerini [2002] for a keynote and a tutorial. Relationships between data exchange and integration have also been explored [Giacomo et al., 2007].

CHAPTER 2

Relational Mappings and Data Exchange

2.1 RELATIONAL DATABASES: KEY DEFINITIONS

In Chapter 1, we presented the key definitions related to data exchange in the most general setting. We now restate these definitions in the context of *relational* data exchange, and recall some key concepts from relational database theory.

2.1.1 RELATIONAL SCHEMAS AND CONSTRAINTS

A *relational schema* **R** is a finite sequence $\langle U_1, \ldots, U_m \rangle$ of relation symbols, with each U_i having a fixed arity $n_i > 0$. For example, the target relational schema considered in the introduction has three relations: ROUTES of arity 3, INFO_FLIGHT of arity 4, and SERVES, also of arity 4.

We sometimes consider relational schemas with *integrity constraints*, which are conditions that instances of such schemas must satisfy. The most commonly used constraints in databases are functional dependencies (and a special case of those: keys) and inclusion dependencies (and a special case of functional and inclusion dependencies: foreign keys).

A functional dependency states that a set of attributes X uniquely determines another set of attributes Y; a key states that a set of attributes uniquely determines the tuple. For example, it is reasonable to assume that flight# is a key of ROUTES, which one may write as a logical sentence

$$\forall f \forall s \forall d \forall s' \forall d' \, \big(\text{ROUTES}(f, s, d) \wedge \text{ROUTES}(f, s', d') \ \rightarrow \ (s = s') \wedge (d = d')\big).$$

An inclusion dependency states that a value of an attribute (or values of a set of attributes) occurring in one relation must occur in another relation as well. For example, we may expect each flight number appearing in INFO_FLIGHT to appear in ROUTES as well: this is expressed as a logical sentence

$$\forall f \forall d \forall a \forall a' \, \big(\text{INFO\_FLIGHT}(f, d, a, a') \ \rightarrow \ \exists s \exists d' \, \text{ROUTES}(f, s, d')\big).$$

Foreign keys are simply a combination of an inclusion dependency and a key constraint: by combining the above inclusion dependency with the constraint that flight# is a key for ROUTES, we get a foreign key constraint INFO_FLIGHT[flight#] $\subseteq_{\text{FK}}$ ROUTES[flight#], stating that each value of flight number in INFO_FLIGHT occurs in ROUTES, and that this value is an identifier for the tuple in ROUTES.

2.1.2   INSTANCES, CONSTANTS, AND NULLS

An *instance* S of schema $\mathbf{R} = \langle U_1, \ldots, U_m \rangle$ assigns to each relation symbol U_i, where $1 \leq i \leq m$, a finite n_i-ary relation U_i^S. The *domain* of instance S, denoted by $\mathrm{DOM}(S)$, is the set of all elements that occur in any of the relations U_i^S. It is often convenient to define instances by simply listing the tuples attached to the corresponding relation symbols. Further, sometimes we use the notation $U(\bar{t}) \in S$ instead of $\bar{t} \in U^S$, and call $U(\bar{t})$ a *fact* of S. For instance, FLIGHT(*Paris, Santiago, AirFrance*, 2320) is an example of a fact. Finally, given instances S, S' of $\mathbf{R}$, we denote by $S \subseteq S'$ the fact that $U_i^S \subseteq U_i^{S'}$ for every $i \in \{1, \ldots, m\}$, and we denote by $\|S\|$ the size of S.

We have seen in earlier examples that target instances may contain *incomplete information*. This is modeled by having two disjoint and infinite set of values that populate instances. One of them is the set of *constants*, denoted by Const, and the other one is the set of *nulls*, or variables, denoted by Var. In general, the domain of an instance is a subset of Const $\cup$ Var (although we shall assume that domains of a source instances are always contained in Const). We usually denote constants by lowercase letters $a, b, c, \ldots$, while nulls are denoted by symbols $\perp, \perp_1, \perp_2$, etc.

We now need a couple of standard definitions related to database instances with nulls. Given an instance S of schema $\mathbf{R}$, let V be the set of all nulls that occur in S. We then call a mapping $v : V \to$ Const a *valuation*. By $v(S)$, we mean the instance obtained from S by changing every occurrence of a null $\perp$ by $v(\perp)$. Then

$$Rep(S) \quad = \quad \{S' \text{ over Const} \mid v(S) \subseteq S' \text{ for some valuation } v\}$$

is the set of instances over Const represented by S. This notion is typically viewed as the semantics of an incomplete instance S with nulls: such an instance may represent several complete instances depending on the evaluation of nulls, and possibly adding new tuples.

2.2   RELATIONAL SCHEMA MAPPINGS

Following the terminology used in Chapter 1, we define a *relational mapping* $\mathcal{M}$ as a tuple $(\mathbf{R_s}, \mathbf{R_t}, \Sigma_{st}, \Sigma_t)$, where $\mathbf{R_s}$ and $\mathbf{R_t}$ are disjoint relational schemas, $\mathbf{R_s}$ is called the *source* schema, $\mathbf{R_t}$ is called the *target* schema, Σ_{st} is a finite set of *source-to-target* dependencies (i.e., dependencies over the relations in $\mathbf{R_s}$ and $\mathbf{R_t}$), and Σ_t is a finite set of *target* dependencies (i.e., dependencies over $\mathbf{R_t}$). If the set Σ_t is empty, i.e., there are no target dependencies, we write $\mathcal{M} = (\mathbf{R_s}, \mathbf{R_t}, \Sigma_{st})$.

Recall that instances of $\mathbf{R_s}$ are called *source* instances, while instances of $\mathbf{R_t}$ are called *target* instances. Source instances are usually denoted $S, S_1, S_2, \ldots$, while target instances are denoted $T, T_1, T_2, \ldots$

To define the notion of a solution we need the following terminology. Given schemas $\mathbf{R_1} = \langle U_1, \ldots, U_m \rangle$ and $\mathbf{R_2} = \langle W_1, \ldots, W_n \rangle$, with no relation symbols in common, we denote by $\langle \mathbf{R_1}, \mathbf{R_2} \rangle$ the schema $\langle U_1, \ldots, U_m, W_1, \ldots, W_n \rangle$. Further, if S_1 is an instance of $\mathbf{R_1}$ and S_2 is an instance of $\mathbf{R_2}$, then (S_1, S_2) denotes an instance T of $\langle \mathbf{R_1}, \mathbf{R_2} \rangle$ such that $U_i^T = U_i^{S_1}$ and $W_j^T = W_j^{S_2}$, for each $i \in \{1, \ldots, m\}$ and $j \in \{1, \ldots, n\}$.

Given a source instance S over $\texttt{Const}$, we say that a target instance T over $\texttt{Const} \cup \texttt{Var}$ is a *solution for S under* $\mathcal{M}$, if (S, T) satisfies every sentence in Σ_{st} and T satisfies every sentence in Σ_t. In symbols, $(S, T) \models \Sigma_{st}$ and $T \models \Sigma_t$. When $\mathcal{M}$ is clear from the context, we say call T simply a solution for S. As before, the set of solutions for instance S will be denoted by $\text{Sol}_{\mathcal{M}}(S)$.

Admitting arbitrary expressive power for specifying dependencies in data exchange easily leads to undecidability of some fundamental problems, like checking for the existence of solutions. Thus, it is customary in the data exchange literature to restrict the study to a class of mappings $\mathcal{M}$ that lead to efficient decidability of the key computational tasks associated with data exchange. The standard restrictions used in data exchange are as follows: constraints used in Σ_{st} are *tuple-generating dependencies* (which generalize inclusion dependencies), and constraints in Σ_t are either tuple-generating dependencies or *equality-generating dependencies* (which generalize functional dependencies). More precisely:

- Σ_{st} consists of a set of *source-to-target tuple-generating dependencies (st-tgds)* of the form

$$\forall \bar{x} \forall \bar{y} \, (\varphi_s(\bar{x}, \bar{y}) \rightarrow \exists \bar{z} \, \psi_t(\bar{x}, \bar{z})),$$

where $\varphi_s(\bar{x}, \bar{y})$ and $\psi_t(\bar{x}, \bar{z})$ are conjunctions of atomic formulas in $\mathbf{R_s}$ and $\mathbf{R_t}$, respectively; and

- Σ_t is the union of a set of *tuple-generating dependencies (tgds)*, i.e., dependencies of the form

$$\forall \bar{x} \forall \bar{y} \, (\varphi(\bar{x}, \bar{y}) \rightarrow \exists \bar{z} \, \psi(\bar{x}, \bar{z})),$$

where $\varphi(\bar{x}, \bar{y})$ and $\psi(\bar{x}, \bar{z})$ are conjunctions of atomic formulas in $\mathbf{R_t}$, and a set of *equality-generating dependencies (egds)*, i.e., dependencies of the form

$$\forall \bar{x} \, (\varphi(\bar{x}) \rightarrow x_i = x_j),$$

where $\varphi(\bar{x})$ is a conjunction of atomic formulas in $\mathbf{R_t}$, and x_i, x_j are variables among those in $\bar{x}$.

One can observe that the mapping we used in the Introduction follows this pattern. For the sake of simplicity, we usually omit universal quantification in front of st-tgds, tgds, and egds. Notice, in addition, that each (st-)tgd $\varphi(\bar{x}, \bar{y}) \rightarrow \exists \bar{z} \, \psi(\bar{x}, \bar{z})$ is logically equivalent to the formula $(\exists \bar{y} \, \varphi(\bar{x}, \bar{y})) \rightarrow (\exists \bar{z} \, \psi(\bar{x}, \bar{z}))$. Thus, when we use notation $\theta(\bar{x}) \rightarrow \exists \bar{z} \, \psi(\bar{x}, \bar{z})$ for a (st-)tgd, we assume that $\theta(\bar{x})$ is a formula of the form $\exists \bar{y} \, \varphi(\bar{x}, \bar{y})$, where $\varphi(\bar{x}, \bar{y})$ is a conjunction of atomic formulas. Also, we denote by $\|\mathcal{M}\|$ the size of a mapping $\mathcal{M}$.

From now on, and unless stated otherwise, we assume all relational mappings to be of the restricted form specified above. The intuition behind the different components of these mappings is as follows. Source-to-target dependencies in Σ_{st} are a tool for specifying which conditions on the source imply a condition on the target. But from a different point of view, one can also see them as a tool for specifying how source data gets translated into target data. In addition, the translated data must satisfy usual database constraints. This is represented by means of the target dependencies in Σ_t. It is important to notice that the mappings described above are not restrictive from a database point of view. Indeed, tuple-generating dependencies together with equality generating dependencies precisely capture the class of *embedded* dependencies. And the latter class contains all relevant dependencies that appear in relational databases, e.g., it contains functional and inclusion dependencies, among others.

There is a particular class of data exchange mappings, called *Local-As-View* (LAV) mappings, that often appears in the literature. This class had its origins in the data integration community, but it has proved to be of interest also for data exchange. Formally, a mapping without target constraints $\mathcal{M} = (\mathbf{R_s}, \mathbf{R_t}, \Sigma_{st})$ is a LAV mapping if Σ_{st} consists of LAV st-tgds of the form $\forall \bar{x}(U(\bar{x}) \rightarrow \exists \bar{z}\, \varphi_t(\bar{x}, \bar{z}))$, where U is a relation symbol in $\mathbf{R_s}$. That is, to generate tuples in the target, one needs a single source fact.

2.3   MATERIALIZING TARGET INSTANCES

As we mentioned in Chapter 1, one of the key goals in data exchange is to materialize a solution that reflects as accurately as possible the given source instance. The next example shows two interesting phenomena regarding solutions in data exchange that, in particular, explain why the materialization problem is far from trivial. First, solutions for a given source instance are not necessarily unique. Second, there are source instances that have no solutions.

Example 2.1   Let us revisit the data exchange example presented in Chapter 1. Thus, $\mathcal{M} = (\mathbf{R_s}, \mathbf{R_t}, \Sigma_{st}, \Sigma_t)$ is a mapping such that:

- The source schema $\mathbf{R_s}$ consists of the ternary relation

$$\texttt{GEO(city,country,population)}$$

  and the 4-ary relation

$$\texttt{FLIGHT(source,destination,airline,departure)}.$$

- The target schema $\mathbf{R_t}$ consists of the ternary relation

$$\texttt{ROUTES(flight\#,source,destination)}$$

  and the 4-ary relations

$$\texttt{INFO\_FLIGHT(flight\#,departure\_time,arrival\_time,airline)}$$
$$\text{and}$$
$$\texttt{SERVES(airline,city,country,phone)}.$$

- Σ_{st} consists of the following st-tgds:

  ```
  FLIGHT(src,dest,airl,dep) ⟶
      ∃f#∃arr (ROUTES(f#,src,dest) ∧ INFO_FLIGHT(f#,dep,arr,airl))

  FLIGHT(city,dest,airl,dep) ∧ GEO(city,country,popul) ⟶
          ∃phone SERVES(airl,city,country,phone)

  FLIGHT(src,city,airl,dep) ∧ GEO(city,country,popul) ⟶
          ∃phone SERVES(airl,city,country,phone).
  ```

- There are no target dependencies, i.e., $\Sigma_t = \emptyset$.

It is clear that every source instance has a solution under $\mathcal{M}$. Furthermore, since the st-tgds do not completely specify the target, solutions are not necessarily unique up to isomorphism, and, indeed, there is an infinite number of solutions for each source instance.

On the other hand, assume that $\mathcal{M}'$ is the extension of $\mathcal{M}$ with the target dependency that imposes that src is a key in ROUTES(f#,src,dest). Then it is no longer true that every source instance has a solution under $\mathcal{M}'$. Indeed, consider a source instance S that contains facts FLIGHT(*Paris, Santiago, AirFrance*, 2320) and FLIGHT(*Paris, Rio, TAM*, 1720). Then the first st-tgd in Σ_{st} imposes that there are facts of the form ROUTES(x, *Paris, Santiago*) and ROUTES(y, *Paris, Rio*) in every solution T for S. But this contradicts the key condition on relation Routes(f#,src,dest). We conclude that S has no solutions under $\mathcal{M}'$. □

This example suggests that in order to be able to materialize a target solution for a given source instance, we have to be able to do two things. First, to determine whether a solution exists at all; and second, in case that there is more than just one solution, to compute the one that reflects most accurately the source data. Each one of these issues is naturally associated with a relevant data exchange problem.

- First, in order to determine whether solutions exist, it is necessary to understand the decidability of the problem of checking for the existence of solutions, as defined below:

PROBLEM:	Existence of solutions for relational mapping $\mathcal{M}$.
INPUT:	A source instance S.
QUESTION:	Is there a solution for S under $\mathcal{M}$?

- Second, it is necessary to identify the class of data exchange solutions that most accurately reflect the source data and to understand the computability of the solutions in this class.

This section is devoted to the study of these two problems. First, it is shown in Section 2.3.1 that, in the more general scenario, the existence of solutions problem is undecidable. Second, in Section

2.3.2 we present a class of solutions, called *universal solutions*, that are widely assumed to be the preferred solutions in data exchange. Unfortunately, as we point out below, universal solutions are not a general phenomenon in data exchange as there are source instances that have solutions but no universal solutions.

The two previous facts raise the need for identifying a relevant class of relational mappings that satisfies the following desiderata:

(C1) The existence of solutions implies the existence of universal solutions;

(C2) checking the existence of solutions is a decidable (ideally, tractable) problem; and

(C3) for every source instance that has a solution, at least one universal solution can be computed (hopefully, in polynomial time).

The definition of such a class is given in Section 2.3.3. Finally, Section 2.3.4 is devoted to the study of a particular universal solution, called the core, which exhibits good properties for data exchange.

2.3.1   EXISTENCE OF SOLUTIONS

As we have mentioned on and on, one of the goals in data exchange is materializing a solution that reflects as accurately as possible the source data. Unfortunately, even the most basic problem of checking the existence of solutions (for a fixed mapping) is undecidable.

Theorem 2.2   *There exists a relational mapping* $\mathcal{M} = (\mathbf{R_s}, \mathbf{R_t}, \Sigma_{st}, \Sigma_t)$, *such that the problem of checking whether a given source instance has a solution under* $\mathcal{M}$, *is undecidable.*

Proof. We reduce from the embedding problem for finite semi-groups (explained below), which is known to be undecidable.

Recall that a finite semi-group is an algebra $\mathbf{A} = (A, f)$, where A is a finite nonempty set and f is an associative binary function on A. Let $\mathbf{B} = (B, g)$ be a partial finite algebra; i.e., B is a finite nonempty set and g is a partial function from $B \times B$ to B. Then $\mathbf{B}$ is *embeddable* in the finite semi-group $\mathbf{A} = (A, f)$ if and only if $B \subseteq A$ and f is an extension of g, that is, whenever $g(a, a')$ is defined, we have that $g(a, a') = f(a, a')$. The *embedding* problem for finite semi-groups is as follows: given a finite partial algebra $\mathbf{B} = (B, g)$, is $\mathbf{B}$ embeddable in some finite semi-group?

We now construct a relational mapping $\mathcal{M} = (\mathbf{R_s}, \mathbf{R_t}, \Sigma_{st}, \Sigma_t)$ such that the embedding problem for finite semi-groups is reducible to the problem of existence of solutions for $\mathcal{M}$. The mapping $\mathcal{M}$ is constructed as follows:

- $\mathbf{R_s}$ consists of the ternary relation symbol U, while $\mathbf{R_t}$ consists of the ternary relation symbol V. Intuitively, both U and V encode the graphs of binary functions.

- $\Sigma_{st} = \{U(x, y, z) \rightarrow V(x, y, z)\}$.

- Σ_t consists of one egd and two tgds. First, an egd

$$V(x, y, z) \wedge V(x, y, z') \to z = z',$$

asserts that V encodes a function. Second, a tgd

$$V(x, y, u) \wedge V(y, z, v) \wedge V(u, z, w) \to V(x, v, w),$$

that asserts that the function encoded by V is associative. Finally, a tgd

$$V(x_1, x_2, x_3) \wedge V(y_1, y_2, y_3) \to \bigwedge_{1 \le i,j \le 3} \exists z_{ij} \, V(x_i, y_j, z_{ij})$$

that states that the function encoded by V is total. Indeed, this tgd expresses that if two elements a and b appear in the interpretation of V, then there must be an element c such that $V(a, b, c)$.

Let $\mathbf{B} = (B, g)$ be a finite partial algebra. Consider the source instance $S_{\mathbf{B}} = \{U(a, b, c) \mid g(a, b) = c\}$. It is clear that $\mathbf{B}$ is embeddable in the class of finite semi-groups if and only if $S_{\mathbf{B}}$ has a solution under $\mathcal{M}$. This shows that the existence of solutions problem for $\mathcal{M}$ is undecidable. $\square$

2.3.2   UNIVERSAL SOLUTIONS

As we have mentioned above, we want to identify which data exchange solutions better reflect the source data. As it is widely accepted in the data exchange literature, this corresponds to the class of *universal* solutions. Intuitively, a solution is universal when it is more *general* than any other solution. Next example will help us to illustrate when a solution is more general than other.

Example 2.3   (Example 2.1 continued)   Consider the source instance

$$S = \{\text{FLIGHT}(Paris, Santiago, AirFrance, 2320)\}.$$

Then one possible solution for S under $\mathcal{M}$ is

$$T = \{\text{ROUTES}(\perp_1, Paris, Santiago), \text{INFO\_FLIGHT}(\perp_1, 2320, \perp_2, AirFrance)\},$$

where $\perp_1, \perp_2$ are values in Var (i.e., nulls). Another solution is

$$T' = \{\text{ROUTES}(\perp_1, Paris, Santiago), \text{INFO\_FLIGHT}(\perp_1, 2320, \perp_1, AirFrance)\}.$$

Yet another solution, but with no nulls, is

$$T'' = \{\text{ROUTES}(AF406, Paris, Santiago),$$
$$\text{INFO\_FLIGHT}(AF406, 2320, 920, AirFrance)\}.$$

Notice that both solutions T' and T'' seem to be less general than T. This is because T' assumes that the values that witness the existentially quantified variables $\text{f\#}$ and arr, in the first st-tgd of Σ_{st}, are the same, while T'' assumes that these variables are witnessed by the constants $AF406$ and 920, respectively. On the other hand, solution T contains exactly what the specification requires. Thus, in this case it seems natural to say that one would like to materialize a solution like T rather than solution T' or T'', as T is more accurate with respect to S (under $\mathcal{M}$) than T' and T''.   □

How do we define the notion of being as general as any other solution? There appear to be three different ways of doing so, outlined below.

Solutions that describe all others. A solution T is an instance with nulls, and thus describes the set $Rep(T)$ of complete solutions. A most general solution must describe all other complete solutions: that is, we must have

$$\textbf{UnivSol}_1(T): \qquad Rep(T) \;=\; \{T' \in \text{Sol}_{\mathcal{M}}(S) \mid T' \text{ is over } \texttt{Const}\}$$

Solutions that are as general as others. A seemingly slightly weaker condition says that if a solution T is universal, it cannot describe fewer complete instances than another solution, i.e.,

$$\textbf{UnivSol}_2(T): \qquad Rep(T') \subseteq Rep(T) \text{ for every } T' \in \text{Sol}_{\mathcal{M}}(S)$$

Solutions that map homomorphically into others. This more technical, and yet very convenient definition, is inspired by the algebraic notion of a universal object, that has a homomorphism into every object in a class. A *homomorphism* between two instances $h : T \to T'$ is a mapping from the domain of T into the domain of T', that is the identity on constants, and such that $\bar{t} = (t_1, \ldots, t_n) \in W^T$ implies $h(\bar{t}) = (h(t_1), \ldots, h(t_n))$ is in $W^{T'}$ for all W in $\mathbf{R_t}$. Our third condition then is:

$$\textbf{UnivSol}_3(T): \qquad \text{there is a homomorphism } h : T \to T' \text{ for every } T' \in \text{Sol}_{\mathcal{M}}(S)$$

So, which definition should we adopt? It turns out that we can take either one, as they are equivalent.

Proposition 2.4   *If $\mathcal{M}$ is a mapping given by st-tgds, and T is a solution for some source instance, then conditions $\textbf{UnivSol}_1(T)$, $\textbf{UnivSol}_2(T)$, and $\textbf{UnivSol}_3(T)$ are equivalent.*

Proof. Observe that a valuation ν on T is a homomorphism from T into any instance containing $\nu(T)$. Since right-hand-sides of st-tgds are conjunctive queries, which are closed under homomorphisms, we have that if $T \in \text{Sol}_{\mathcal{M}}(S)$ and $T' \in Rep(T)$, then $T' \in \text{Sol}_{\mathcal{M}}(S)$. With this observation, we now easily prove the result.

$\textbf{UnivSol}_1(T) \Rightarrow \textbf{UnivSol}_2(T)$. Assume T' is an arbitrary solution, and let $T'' \in Rep(T')$. Then T'' is a solution without nulls, and hence by $\textbf{UnivSol}_1(T)$ it belongs to $Rep(T)$, proving $Rep(T') \subseteq Rep(T)$.

UnivSol$_2$(T) $\Rightarrow$ UnivSol$_3$(T). Let $T' \in \text{Sol}_{\mathcal{M}}(S)$, and let $\perp_1, \ldots, \perp_n$ enumerate nulls in T'. Let $c_1, \ldots, c_n$ be elements of Const that do not occur in T', and let T'' be obtained from T' by replacing each $\perp_i$ with c_i, for $i \leq n$. Then $T'' \in Rep(T')$ and hence $T'' \in Rep(T)$. Take a valuation v witnessing $T'' \in Rep(T)$ and change it into a homomorphism by setting $h(\perp) = \perp_i$ whenever $v(\perp) = c_i$, and otherwise letting h coincide with v. Then clearly h is a homomorphism from T to T'.

UnivSol$_3$(T) $\Rightarrow$ UnivSol$_1$(T). If $T' \in Rep(T)$, we know it is a solution. On the other hand, if T' is a solution over constants, then there is a homomorphism $h : T \to T'$, which must be a valuation since there are no nulls in T'. Hence $T' \in Rep(T)$. This completes the proof of the proposition. □

Proposition 2.4 justifies the following definition.

Definition 2.5 (Universal solutions). Given a mapping $\mathcal{M}$, a solution T for S under $\mathcal{M}$ is a *universal* solution if one of **UnivSol$_i$(T)**, for $i = 1, 2, 3$, is satisfied (and hence all are satisfied). □

Most commonly in the proofs one uses the condition that for every solution T' for S, there exists a homomorphism $h : T \to T'$.

Example 2.6 Neither solution T' nor T'' in Example 2.3 is universal. In fact, there is no homomorphism $h : T' \to T$; otherwise

$$h((\perp_1, 2320, \perp_1, AirFrance)) = (\perp_1, 2320, \perp_2, AirFrance),$$

and, thus, $h(\perp_1) = \perp_1$ and $h(\perp_1) = \perp_2$, which is a contradiction. Moreover, there is no homomorphism $h : T'' \to T$; otherwise

$$h((AF406, 2320, 920, AirFrance)) = (\perp_1, 2320, \perp_2, AirFrance),$$

and, thus, $h(AF406) = \perp_1$ and $h(920) = \perp_2$, which is a contradiction (because homomorphisms are the identity on constants). On the other hand, it can be easily seen that T is a universal solution. □

In addition to being more general than arbitrary solutions, universal solutions possess many good properties that justify materializing them (as opposed to arbitrary solutions). We shall study these properties in detail in this chapter. Unfortunately, universal solutions are not a general phenomenon. Indeed, it can be proved that there is a mapping $\mathcal{M}$ and a source instance S, such that S has at least one solution under $\mathcal{M}$ but has no universal solutions (see Example 2.11). Thus, it is necessary to impose extra conditions on dependencies if one wants to ensure that the existence of solutions implies the existence of universal solutions. We study this issue in the next section.

2.3.3   MATERIALIZING UNIVERSAL SOLUTIONS

Summing up, for arbitrary relational mappings we have two negative results: the existence of solutions problem is undecidable, and the existence of solutions does not always imply the existence of universal solutions. Thus, one would like to restrict the class of dependencies allowed in mappings, in such a way that it satisfies the following:

(C1) The existence of solutions implies the existence of universal solutions;

(C2) checking the existence of solutions is a decidable (ideally, tractable) problem; and

(C3) for every source instance that has a solution, at least one universal solution can be computed (hopefully, in polynomial time).

But before looking for such a class it is convenient to talk about the main algorithmic tool that the data exchange community has applied in order to check for the existence of solutions; the well-known *chase* procedure, that was originally designed to reason about the implication problem for data dependencies. In data exchange, the chase is used as a tool for constructing a universal solution for a given source instance. The basic idea is the following. The chase starts with the source instance S, and then triggers every dependency in $\Sigma_{st} \cup \Sigma_t$, as long as this process is applicable. In doing so, the chase may fail (if firing an egd forces two constants to be equal) or it may never terminate (for instance, in some cases when the set of tgds is *cyclic*).

We first define the notion of chase *step* for an instance S. We distinguish between two kinds of chase steps:

(tgd) Let d be a tgd of the form $\varphi(\bar{x}) \rightarrow \exists \bar{z}\, \psi(\bar{x}, \bar{z})$, such that for some tuple $\bar{a}$ of elements in S it is the case that $\varphi(\bar{a})$ holds in S, where $|\bar{a}| = |\bar{x}|$. Then the *result of applying d to S with $\bar{a}$* is the instance S' that extends S with every fact $R(\bar{c})$ that belongs to $\psi(\bar{a}, \bar{\perp})$, where $\bar{\perp}$ is a tupe of fresh distinct values in $\mathtt{Var}$ such that $|\bar{\perp}| = |\bar{z}|$.

In that case we write $S \xrightarrow{d,(\bar{a},\bar{b})} S'$.

(egd) Let d be an egd of the form $\varphi(\bar{x}) \rightarrow x_1 = x_2$, and assume that for some tuple $\bar{a}$ of elements in S it is the case that (1) $\varphi(\bar{a})$ holds in S, and (2) if a_1 is the element of $\bar{a}$ corresponding to x_1 and a_2 is the element of $\bar{a}$ corresponding to x_2, then $a_1 \neq a_2$. We have to consider two cases:

   – If both a_1 and a_2 are constants, the *result of applying d to S with $\bar{a}$* is "failure", which is denoted by $S \xrightarrow{d,\bar{a}} \mathtt{fail}$.

   – Otherwise, the *result of applying d to S with $\bar{a}$* is the instance S' such that the following holds: If one of a_1 or a_2 is a constant c and the other one is a null $\perp$, then S' is obtained from S by replacing every occurrence of $\perp$ in S by c; if, on the other hand, a_1 and a_2 are nulls, then S' is obtained from S by replacing each occurrence of one of those nulls by the other one. In both cases we write $S \xrightarrow{d,\bar{a}} S'$.

With the notion of chase step we can now define what is a chase sequence.

Definition 2.7   (Chase).   Let Σ be a set of tgds and egds and S be an instance.

- A chase *sequence* for S under Σ is a sequence $S_i \xrightarrow{d_i, \bar{a}_i} S_{i+1}$ of chase steps, $i \geq 0$, such that $S_0 = S$, each d_i is a dependency in Σ, and for each distinct $i, j \geq 0$, it is the case that $(d_i, \bar{a}_i) \neq (d_j, \bar{a}_j)$ (that is, $d_i \neq d_j$ or $\bar{a}_i \neq \bar{a}_j$). This last technical condition ensures that chase sequences consist of different chase steps.

- A *finite* chase sequence for S under $\mathcal{M}$ is a chase sequence $S_i \xrightarrow{d_i, \bar{a}_i} S_{i+1}, 0 \leq i < m$, for S under $\mathcal{M}$ such that either (1) $S_m = \mathtt{fail}$, or (2) no chase step can be applied to S_m with the dependencies in Σ. Technically, (2) means the following: there is no dependency d in Σ, tuple $\bar{a}$ in S and instance S' such that $S_m \xrightarrow{d, \bar{a}} S'$ and $(d, \bar{a}) \neq (d_i, \bar{a}_i)$ for every $i \in \{0, \ldots, m-1\}$. If $S_m = \mathtt{fail}$, we refer to this sequence as a *failing* chase sequence. Otherwise, we refer to it as a *successful* chase sequence, and we call S_m its *result*.

$\square$

In principle there could be different results of the chase, as we have to make some arbitrary choices: for example, if an egd equates nulls $\bot$ and $\bot'$, we can either replace $\bot$ by $\bot'$, or $\bot'$ by $\bot$. However, it is not hard to see that if T and T' are two results of the chase on S under $\mathcal{M}$, then T and T' are *isomorphic*, i.e., T can be obtained from T' by a renaming of nulls.

Let us now study the application of the chase in a data exchange scenario. Let $\mathcal{M}$ be a relational mapping and S a source instance. A chase sequence for S under $\mathcal{M}$ is defined as a chase sequence for $(S, \emptyset)$ under $\Sigma_{st} \cup \Sigma_t$. Notice that, by definition, any result of a successful chase sequence for S under $\mathcal{M}$ must be an instance of the form (S, T) where T is a solution for S. But not only that, we show in the following theorem that if (S, T) is the result of a successful chase sequence for S under $\mathcal{M}$, then T is a universal solution for S under $\mathcal{M}$. Moreover, we also show in the following theorem that if there exists a failing chase sequence for S under $\mathcal{M}$, then all of its chase sequences are failing, which further implies that S has no solutions under $\mathcal{M}$.

Theorem 2.8   *Let $\mathcal{M}$ be a mapping and S a source instance. If there is a successful chase sequence for S under $\mathcal{M}$ with result (S, T), then T is a universal solution for S. On the other hand, if there exists a failing chase sequence for S under $\mathcal{M}$, then S has no solution.*

Proof.   In order to prove the theorem we need the following technical, but rather intuitive lemma. The proof is left as an exercise.

Lemma 2.9   *Let $S_1 \xrightarrow{d, \bar{a}} S_2$ be a chase step, where $S_2 \neq \mathtt{fail}$. Assume that S_3 is an instance that satisfies the dependency d and such that there is a homomorphism from S_1 into S_3. Then there exists a homomorphism from S_2 into S_3.*

We now prove the theorem. Assume first that (S, T) is the result of a successful chase sequence for S under $\mathcal{M}$. Then, as we mentioned above, T is a solution for S. We show next that it is also a universal solution. Let T' be an arbitrary solution for S. Thus, (S, T') satisfies every dependency in $\Sigma_{st} \cup \Sigma_t$. Furthermore, the identity mapping is a homomorphism from $(S, \emptyset)$ into (S, T'). Applying Lemma 2.9 at each step of the chase sequence with result (S, T), we conclude that there exists a homomorphism $h : (S, T) \to (S, T')$. Further, h is also a homomorphism from T into T'.

Assume, on the other hand, that there is a failing chase sequence for S under $\mathcal{M}$, and that the last chase step in that sequence is $(S, T) \xrightarrow{d, \bar{a}} \texttt{fail}$. Thus, d is an egd of the form $\varphi(\bar{x}) \to x_1 = x_2$, $\varphi(\bar{a})$ holds in (S, T), and if a_i is the element corresponding to x_i in $\bar{a}$, $i \in [1, 2]$, then a_1 and a_2 are constants and $a_1 \neq a_2$. Assume, for the sake of contradiction, that S has a solution T'. As in the previous case, it can be proved (with the help of Lemma 2.9) that there is a homomorphism h from T to T'. Thus, $\varphi(h(\bar{a}))$ holds in T', and $h(a_1) = a_1$ and $h(a_2) = a_2$ are distinct constants. This contradicts the fact that T' satisfies d. $\qquad\square$

The result of a successful chase sequence on a source instance S is usually called a *canonical* universal solution for S. Since for the chase as defined in this chapter this result is unique up to isomorphism, in what follows we refer to it as the *canonical* universal solution for S.

Example 2.10   (Example 2.3 continued)   It is clear that the result of the chase for S under $\mathcal{M}$ is T. Thus, from Theorem 2.8, T is a universal solution for S. $\qquad\square$

But the chase as a tool for data exchange has one big drawback: nothing can be concluded about the existence of solutions in the case when the chase does not terminate. The next example shows different applications of the chase procedure.

Example 2.11   Let $\mathcal{M}$ be a mapping such that the source schema consists of a binary relation E, the target schema consists of binary relations G and L, and Σ_{st} consists of the st-tgd $\varphi = E(x, y) \to G(x, y)$. Assume first that Σ_t consists of the tgd $\theta_1 = G(x, y) \to \exists z\, L(y, z)$, and let S be the source instance $E(a, b)$. The chase starts by firing φ and, thus, by populating the target with the fact $G(a, b)$. In a second stage, the chase realizes that θ_1 is being violated, and thus, θ_1 is triggered. The target is then extended with a fact $L(b, \bot)$, where $\bot$ is a fresh null value. At this stage, no dependency is being violated, and thus, the chase stops with result $T = \{G(a, b), L(b, \bot)\}$. We conclude that T is a universal solution for S.

Assume now that Σ_t is extended with the tgd $\theta_2 = L(x, y) \to \exists z\, G(y, z)$. Clearly, T does not satisfy θ_2 and the chase triggers this tgd. This means that a fact $G(\bot, \bot_1)$ is added to the target, where $\bot_1$ is a fresh null value. But θ_1 is now being violated again, and a new fact $L(\bot_1, \bot_2)$, where $\bot_2$ is a fresh null value, will have to be added. It is clear that this process will continue indefinitely, and thus, that the chase does not terminate. Notice that in this case $T = \{G(a, b), L(b, a)\}$ is a solution for S. It can be proved, on the other hand, that S does not have universal solutions. (We leave this as an exercise to the reader).

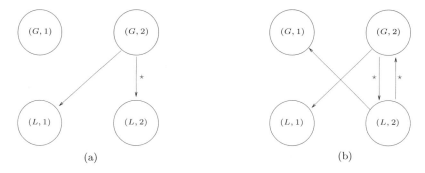

Figure 2.1: Dependency graphs of (a) $\{\theta_1\}$ and (b) $\{\theta_1, \theta_2\}$.

Assume finally that Σ_t consists of the egd $\alpha = G(x, y) \rightarrow x = y$. Then the chase for S fails, since after populating the target instance with the fact $G(a, b)$, the egd α forces to equate the constants a and b. Notice that, in this case, S has no solution. □

As we have seen, the main problem with the application of the chase is non-termination. This happens, for instance, when the set of tgds allows for cascading of null creation during the chase. We show next that by restricting this cascading it is possible to obtain a meaningful class of mappings, for which the chase is guaranteed to terminate; further, it does so in at most polynomially many steps. It will follow that this class of mappings satisfies our desiderata expressed above as conditions C1, C2 and C3.

Assume that Σ is a set of tgds over $\mathbf{R_t}$. We construct the *dependency* graph of Σ as follows. The nodes (positions) of the graph are all pairs (R, i), where R is a relation symbol in $\mathbf{R_t}$ of arity n and $i \in \{1, \ldots, n\}$. Then we add edges as follows. For every tgd $\forall \bar{x} \forall \bar{y} \, (\varphi(\bar{x}, \bar{y}) \rightarrow \exists \bar{z} \, \psi(\bar{x}, \bar{z}))$ in Σ, and for every variable x mentioned in $\bar{x}$ that occurs in the i-th attribute of relation R in φ, do the following:

- if x occurs in the j-th attribute of relation T in ψ, then add an edge from (R, i) to (T, j) (if the edge does not already exist); and

- for every existentially quantified variable in $\exists \bar{z} \, \psi(\bar{x}, \bar{z})$ that occurs in the j-th attribute of relation T in ψ, add an edge labeled $\star$ from (R, i) to (T, j) (if the edge does not already exist).

Finally, we say that Σ is *weakly acyclic* if the dependency graph of Σ does not have a cycle going through an edge labeled $\star$.

Example 2.12 (Example 2.11 continued)   Let θ_1 and θ_2 be as in Example 2.11. As it is shown in Figure 2.1, the set $\{\theta_1\}$ is weakly acyclic, while the set $\{\theta_1, \theta_2\}$ is not as there is a cycle in the dependency graph of these dependencies going through an edge labeled $\star$. □

Interesting classes of weakly acyclic sets of tgds include the following:

- Sets of tgds without existential quantifiers, and

- *acyclic* sets of inclusion dependencies.

The intuition behind this notion is as follows. Edges labeled $\star$ keep track of positions (R, i) for which the chase will have to create a fresh null value every time the left hand side of the corresponding tgd is triggered. Thus, a cycle through an edge labeled $\star$ implies that a fresh null value created in a position at a certain stage of the chase may determine the creation of another fresh null value, in the same position, at a later stage. Therefore, sets of tgds that are not weakly acyclic may yield non-terminating chase sequences (e.g., the set $\{\theta_1, \theta_2\}$). On the other hand, it can be proved that the chase always terminates for mappings with a weakly acyclic sets of tgds. Further, in this case, the chase for S terminates in at most polynomially many stages.

Theorem 2.13   *Let $\mathcal{M} = (\mathbf{R_s}, \mathbf{R_t}, \Sigma_{st}, \Sigma_t)$ be a fixed relational mapping, such that Σ_t is the union of a set of egds and a weakly acyclic set of tgds. Then there exists a polynomial p such that the length of every chase sequence for a source instance S under $\mathcal{M}$ is bounded by $p(\|S\|)$.*

Proof. For the sake of simplicity, we prove the theorem in the absence of egds. The addition of egds does not change the argument of the proof in any fundamental way.

First of all, with each node (V, i) in the dependency graph of Σ_t, we associate its *rank*, denoted by $rank(V, i)$, which is the maximum number of special edges in any path in the dependency graph G of Σ_{st} that ends in (V, i). Since Σ_{st} is weakly acyclic, the rank of each node in G is finite. Further, it is clear that the maximum rank r of a node in G is bounded by the number m of nodes in G itself. Notice that m (and, thus, r) is a constant since it corresponds to the total number of attributes in the schema $\mathbf{R_t}$ (which is assumed to be fixed).

Let us partition the nodes of G into sets $N_0, N_1, \ldots, N_r$ such that (V, i) belongs to N_j if and only if $rank(V, i) = j$ $(0 \leq j \leq r)$. To prove the theorem, we need the following technical result. (The proof is left as an exercise).

Claim 2.14   *For each $j \in \{1, \ldots, r\}$, there exists a polynomial p_j such that the following holds: Let S be a source instance and T be any target instance that is obtained from S by a sequence of chase steps using the tgds in $\Sigma_{st} \cup \Sigma_t$. Then the number of distinct elements (i.e., constants and nulls) that occur in T at positions that are restricted to be in N_j is bounded by $p_j(\|S\|)$.*

Now it follows from the claim that there exists a polynomial p', that only depends on $\mathcal{M}$, such that the maximum number of elements that occur in a solution T for S under $\mathcal{M}$, at a single position, is bounded by $p'(\|S\|)$. Thus, the total number of tuples that can exist in one relation in T is at most $p'(\|S\|)^m$ (since each relation symbol in $\mathbf{R_t}$ can have arity at most m). Thus, the total number of tuples in T is bounded by $\|\mathcal{M}\| \cdot p'(\|S\|)^m$. This is polynomial in $\|S\|$ since $\mathcal{M}$ is fixed. Furthermore, at each chase step with a tgd at least one tuple is added, which implies that the length of any chase sequence is bounded by $\|\mathcal{M}\| \cdot p'(\|S\|)^m$; hence, we can take $p(x) = \|\mathcal{M}\| \cdot p'(x)^m$. This completes the proof. $\square$

This good behavior also implies the good behavior of this class of mappings with respect to data exchange. Indeed, as an immediate corollary to Theorems 2.8 and 2.13, we obtain the following:

Corollary 2.15   *Let $\mathcal{M} = (\mathbf{R_s}, \mathbf{R_t}, \Sigma_{st}, \Sigma_t)$ be a fixed relational mapping, such that Σ_t is the union of a set of egds, and a weakly acyclic set of tgds. Then the existence of solutions for $\mathcal{M}$ can be checked in polynomial time. Further, in case that solutions exist, a universal solution can be computed in polynomial time.*

Thus, the class of mappings with a weakly acyclic set of tgds satisfies conditions C1, C2, and C3, as defined above, and therefore, it constitutes a good class for data exchange according to our definition. In this case, using the chase the canonical universal solution that can be constructed in polynomial time (if a solution exists at all).

Let us finally mention that there are interesting classes of dependencies for which the problem of checking for the existence of solutions is trivial. For instance, if mappings do not have egds then source instances always have (universal) solutions (under the condition that Σ_t consists of a weakly acyclic set of tgds). In particular, for mappings without target dependencies, it is the case that every source instance has at least one universal solution.

For mappings without target dependencies, the canonical universal solution can always be computed in LOGSPACE. But, as next proposition shows, the complexity increases in the presence of target dependencies (we leave both facts as exercises to the reader):

Proposition 2.16   *There exists a relational mapping $\mathcal{M} = (\mathbf{R_s}, \mathbf{R_t}, \Sigma_{st}, \Sigma_t)$, such that Σ_t consists of a set of tgds without existentially quantified variables, and such that the problem of checking for a given source instance S, whether a fact $R(\bar{t})$ belongs to the canonical universal solution for S, is PTIME-complete.*

On the other hand, the problem of checking for the existence of solutions is PTIME-complete already for mappings whose set of target dependencies consists of a single egd (also left as an exercise to the reader). This means that both the problem of computing the canonical universal solution for mappings with tgds but without egds, and checking for the existence of solutions for mappings with egds but without tgds, are regarded as inherently sequential, and its performance cannot be improved considerably using parallel algorithms.

2.3.4   CORES

We start this section with an example.

Example 2.17   (Example 2.1 continued)   Consider the source instance

$$S = \{\text{FLIGHT}(Paris, Amsterdam, KLM, 1410),$$
$$\text{FLIGHT}(Paris, Amsterdam, KLM, 2230),$$
$$\text{GEO}(Paris, France, 2M)\}.$$

It is not hard to see that the canonical universal solution T for S is

$$\{\text{ROUTES}(\bot_1, Paris, Amsterdam), \text{ROUTES}(\bot_3, Paris, Amsterdam),$$
$$\text{INFO\_FLIGHT}(\bot_1, 1410, \bot_2, KLM), \text{INFO\_FLIGHT}(\bot_3, 2230, \bot_4, KLM),$$
$$\text{SERVES}(KLM, Paris, France, \bot_5), \text{SERVES}(KLM, Paris, France, \bot_6)\}.$$

Now consider the instance T^* that is obtained from T by removing tuple $\text{SERVES}(KLM, Paris, France, \bot_6)$. Then T^* is also a solution for S, and, moreover, there are homomorphisms $h : T \to T^*$ and $h^* : T^* \to T$. It follows, therefore, that T^* is also a universal solution for S. $\qquad\square$

We can draw an interesting conclusion from this example: among all possible universal solutions, the canonical universal solution is not necessarily the smallest (as T^* is strictly contained in T). Moreover, in the example, T^* is actually the smallest universal solution (up to isomorphism).

The first natural question is whether there is always a unique smallest universal solution. As we will see later, this question has a positive answer. Further, some authors have argued that this smallest universal solution is the "best" universal solution since it is the most economical one in terms of size, and that this solution should be the preferred one at the moment of materializing a solution. The whole issue is then how to characterize this smallest universal solution.

It can be shown that the smallest universal solution always coincides with the *core* of the universal solutions. The *core* is a concept that originated in graph theory; here we present it for arbitrary instances.

Definition 2.18   (Core).   Let T be a target instance with values in $\text{Const} \cup \text{Var}$, and let T' be a sub-instance[1] of T. We say that T' is a *core* of T if there is a homomorphism from T to T' (recall that homomorphisms have to be the identity on constants), but there is no homomorphism from T' to a proper sub-instance of itself. $\qquad\square$

The following are well known facts about the cores:

1. every instance has a core, and

---

[1]That is, the domain of T' is contained in the domain of T and $V^{T'} \subseteq V^T$, for every V in $\mathbf{R_t}$. If one of the inclusions is proper, we refer to T' as a *proper sub-instance* of T.

2. all cores of a given instance are isomorphic, i.e., the same up to a renaming of nulls.

Thus, we can talk about *the* core of an instance. To give an intuition behind the second fact, assume that T_1 and T_2 are cores of T, and that $h_i : T \rightarrow T_i$ are homomorphisms, for $i = 1, 2$. Then h_1 restricted to T_2 cannot map it to a substructure of T_1, for otherwise $h_1 \circ h_2$ would be a homomorphism from T to a substructure of the core T_1. Likewise, h_2 restricted to T_1 cannot map it to a substructure of T_2. Hence, these restrictions are one-to-one homomorphisms between T_1 and T_2. From here, it is easy to derive that T_1 and T_2 are isomorphic.

The next result summarizes some of the good properties of cores in data exchange.

Proposition 2.19   *Let $\mathcal{M} = (\mathbf{R_s}, \mathbf{R_t}, \Sigma_{st}, \Sigma_t)$ be a mapping, such that Σ_{st} consists of a set of st–tgds and Σ_t consists of a set of tgds and egds.*

1. *If S is a source instance and T is a universal solution for S, then the core of T is also a universal solution for S.*

2. *If S is a source instance for which a universal solution exists, then every universal solution has the same core (up to a renaming of nulls), and the core of an arbitrary universal solution is precisely the smallest universal solution.*

Example 2.20   (Example 2.17 continued)   The solution T^* is the core of the universal solutions for S since there is a homomorphism from T to T^*, but there is no homomorphism from T^* to a proper sub-instance of itself.   □

In conclusion, the core of the universal solutions has good properties for data exchange. This naturally raises the question about the computability of the core. As we have mentioned, the chase yields a universal solution that is not necessarily the core of the universal solutions, so different techniques have to be applied in order to compute this solution.

It is well-known that computing the core of an arbitrary graph is a computationally intractable problem. Indeed, we know that a graph G is 3-colorable iff there is a homomorphism from G to K_3, the clique of size 3. Thus, G is 3-colorable iff the core of the disjoint union of G and K_3 is K_3 itself. This shows that there is a polynomial time reduction from the problem of 3-colorability into the problem of computing the core of a graph. It follows that the latter is NP-hard. In fact, checking if a *fixed* graph G_0 is the core of an input graph G is an NP-complete problem; if both G and G_0 are inputs, then the complexity is even higher (more precisely, in the class DP, studied in complexity theory).

However, in data exchange, we are interested in computing the core of a universal solution and not of an arbitrary instance. And the intractability of the general problem does not mean bad news in our case. In fact, we are about to see that computing the core of the universal solutions under the class of mappings with a weakly acyclic set of tgds is a tractable problem.

Let us consider first a simple class of relational mappings; those without tgds. Then there is a simple greedy algorithm that computes the core of the universal solutions in case that a universal solution exists. It proceeds as follows. Fix a mapping $\mathcal{M} = (\mathbf{R_s}, \mathbf{R_t}, \Sigma_{st}, \Sigma_t)$ without tgds in Σ_t.

Algorithm 1 COMPUTECORE($\mathcal{M}$)

Require: A source instance S

Ensure: If S has a core under $\mathcal{M}$, then $T^\star$ is a target instance that is a core for S. Otherwise, $T^\star = \texttt{fail}$

1: let T be the result of the chase of S under $\mathcal{M}$
2: **if** $T = \texttt{fail}$ **then**
3:    $T^\star = \texttt{fail}$
4: **else**
5:    $T^\star := T$
6:    **for all** fact $R(\bar{a})$ in $T^\star$ **do**
7:        let $T^{\star,-}$ be an instance obtained from $T^\star$ by removing fact $R(\bar{a})$
8:        **if** $(S, T^{\star,-})$ satisfies Σ_{st} **then**
9:            $T^\star := T^{\star,-}$
10:        **end if**
11:    **end for**
12: **end if**

If the chase computing the canonical universal solution does not fail, then the algorithm outputs the core of the universal solutions for S. Furthermore, this algorithm runs in polynomial time in the size of S.

Unfortunately, the algorithm described above cannot be easily adapted to more complex mappings, and more sophisticated techniques have to be developed if one wants to prove that computation of cores of universal solutions continues being tractable in the presence of tgds. These techniques are based on the *blocks* method described below.

Let us assume for the time being that we deal with mappings without target dependencies. The *blocks* method relies on the following observation. If T is the canonical universal solution of a source instance S with respect to a set of st-tgds Σ_{st}, then the *Gaifman* graph of the nulls of T consists of a set of connected components (blocks) of size bounded by a constant c (this constant depends only on the mapping, that we assume to be fixed). By the Gaifman graph of nulls of T we mean the graph whose nodes are the nulls of T, such that two nulls $\bot_1, \bot_2$ are adjacent iff there is a tuple in some relation of T that mentions both $\bot_1$ and $\bot_2$.

A crucial observation is that checking whether there is a homomorphism from T into an arbitrary instance T' can be done in polynomial time. The justification is that this problem boils down to the problem of whether each block of T has a homomorphism into T'. The latter can be solved in polynomial time since the size of each block is bounded by c. It follows that computing the core of the canonical universal solution T can be done in polynomial time: It is sufficient to check whether there is a homomorphism $h : T \to T$ such that the size of the image of T under h is strictly less than the size of T. Then we replace T by $h(T)$, and iteratively continue this process until reaching a fixed-point.

The blocks method was also extended to the case when Σ_t consists of a set of egds. There is an extra difficulty in this case: The property mentioned above, the bounded block-size in the Gaifman graph of the canonical universal solution T of a source instance S, is no longer true in the presence of egds. This is because the chase, when applied to egds, can equate nulls from different blocks, and thus, create blocks of nulls of arbitrary size. This problem is solved by a surprising rigidity lemma stating the following: Let T be the canonical universal of a source instance with respect to a set of st-tgds Σ_{st}. Further, let T' be the target instance that is obtained from T by chasing with the egds in Σ_t. Then if two nulls $\perp_1$ and $\perp_2$ in different blocks of T are replaced by the same null $\perp$ in T', then $\perp$ is *rigid*. That is, if $h : T' \to T'$ is a homomorphism then $h(\perp) = \perp$, and thus, T' has the bounded block-size property if we treat those nulls as constants.

The situation is much more complex in the presence of tgds. This is because the canonical universal solution T for a source instance S does not have the bounded block-size property, and in addition, it is no longer true that equated nulls are rigid. A refined version of the blocks method has been developed; it was used to show that computing cores of universal solutions for mappings whose set of target dependencies consists of egds and a weakly acyclic set of tgds can be done in polynomial time.

Theorem 2.21   *Let $\mathcal{M} = (\mathbf{R_s}, \mathbf{R_t}, \Sigma_{st}, \Sigma_t)$ be a fixed relational mapping, such that Σ_t consists of a set of egds and a weakly acyclic set of tgds. There is a polynomial-time algorithm that for every source instance S, checks whether a solution for S exists, and if that is the case, computes the core of the universal solutions for S.*

2.4   QUERY ANSWERING

2.4.1   ANSWERING FIRST-ORDER AND CONJUNCTIVE QUERIES

Recall that in the context of data exchange we are interested in computing the certain answers of a query. These are formally defined as follows. Let $\mathcal{M}$ be a relational mapping, Q a query in some query language over the schema $\mathbf{R_t}$, and S a source instance. Then the set of *certain answers of Q with respect to S under $\mathcal{M}$* is

$$certain_{\mathcal{M}}(Q, S) = \bigcap \{Q(T) \mid T \in \textsc{Sol}_{\mathcal{M}}(S)\}.$$

We omit $\mathcal{M}$ if it is clear from the context. If Q is a query of arity 0 (a *Boolean* query), then $certain_{\mathcal{M}}(Q, S) = \texttt{true}$ iff Q is true in every solution T for S; otherwise, $certain_{\mathcal{M}}(Q, S) = \texttt{false}$.

Example 2.22 (Example 2.3 continued)   Consider again the source instance

$$S = \{\text{FLIGHT}(Paris, Santiago, AirFrance, 2320)\}.$$

The certain answers of the query $Q = \text{ROUTES}(x, y, z)$ with respect to S is the empty set. On the other hand, $certain_{\mathcal{M}}(Q', S) = \{(Paris, Santiago)\}$, for $Q' = \exists x\text{ROUTES}(x, y, z)$. □

Given a mapping $\mathcal{M}$ and a query Q over $\mathbf{R_t}$, the problem of computing certain answers for Q under $\mathcal{M}$ is defined as follows:

PROBLEM:	Certain answers for Q and $\mathcal{M}$.
INPUT:	A source instance S and a tuple $\bar{t}$ of elements from S.
QUESTION:	Does $\bar{t}$ belong to $certain_{\mathcal{M}}(Q, S)$?

Evaluating the certain answers of a query involves computing the intersection of a (potentially) infinite number of sets. This strongly suggests that computing certain answers for arbitrary FO queries is an undecidable problem. We can prove this with the help of the mapping $\mathcal{M} = (\mathbf{R_s}, \mathbf{R_t}, \Sigma_{st}, \Sigma_t)$ in Theorem 2.2. Let α be the FO formula that is obtained by taking the conjunction of all dependencies in Σ_t, and let $\mathcal{M}'$ be the mapping that is obtained from $\mathcal{M}$ by removing all target dependencies in Σ_t. Then for every source instance S, we have

$$
\begin{aligned}
certain_{\mathcal{M}'}(\neg\alpha, S) = \texttt{false} \quad &\Leftrightarrow \quad \exists T : T \in \text{Sol}_{\mathcal{M}'}(S) \text{ and } T \not\models \neg\alpha \\
&\Leftrightarrow \quad \exists T : T \in \text{Sol}_{\mathcal{M}'}(S) \text{ and } T \models \alpha \\
&\Leftrightarrow \quad \exists T : T \in \text{Sol}_{\mathcal{M}}(S)
\end{aligned}
$$

Thus, we obtain the following from Theorem 2.2.

Proposition 2.23 *There exists an FO query Q and a mapping $\mathcal{M} = (\mathbf{R_s}, \mathbf{R_t}, \Sigma_{st}, \Sigma_t)$, such that $\Sigma_t = \emptyset$ and the problem of computing certain answers for Q and $\mathcal{M}$ is undecidable.*

This does not preclude, however, the existence of interesting classes of queries for which the problem of computing certain answers is decidable, and even tractable. Indeed, next theorem shows that this is the case for the class of unions of conjunctive queries. Recall that a *conjunctive* query is an FO formula of the form $\exists \bar{x} \, \varphi(\bar{x}, \bar{y})$, where $\varphi(\bar{x}, \bar{y})$ is a conjunction of atoms.

Theorem 2.24 *Let $\mathcal{M} = (\mathbf{R_s}, \mathbf{R_t}, \Sigma_{st}, \Sigma_t)$ be a mapping, such that Σ_t consists of a set of egds and a weakly acyclic set of tgds, and let Q be a union of conjunctive queries. Then the problem of computing certain answers for Q under $\mathcal{M}$ can be solved in polynomial time.*

This is a very positive result since unions of conjunctive queries are very common database queries – they correspond to the *select-project-join-union* fragment of relational algebra and to the core of the standard query language for database systems, SQL.

Theorem 2.24 can be easily proved when we put together the following three facts:

1. Unions of conjunctive queries are preserved under homomorphisms; that is, if Q is a union of conjunctive queries over $\mathbf{R_t}$, T and T' are two target instances such that there is a homomorphism from T to T', and the tuple $\bar{a}$ of constants belongs to the evaluation of Q over T, then $\bar{a}$ also belongs to the evaluation of Q over T';

2. every universal solution can be homomorphically mapped into any other solution, and

3. FO queries, and in particular, unions of conjunctive queries, have polynomial time data complexity.

The actual computation of certain answers is based on the well known concept of *naïve evaluation*. This is a way of evaluating queries over databases that contain nulls. Under naïve evaluation, two steps are performed:

- First, a given query Q is evaluated over an instance T with nulls as if nulls were constants. That is, if $\bot, \bot'$ are nulls and c is a constant, then conditions comparing nulls or nulls and constants are evaluated as follows: $\bot = c$ is false, $\bot = \bot'$ is false, and $\bot = \bot$ is true.

- Second, from the result of the first step, one eliminates all tuples containing nulls. The end result is denoted by $Q_{\downarrow}(T)$.

For example, if we have facts $R(1, \bot)$ and $S(\bot, 2)$, $S(\bot, \bot')$, then the naïve evaluation of the query $Q = \exists z \; R(x, z) \wedge S(z, y)$ results in one tuple $(1, 2)$. Indeed, in the first step one takes the join of R and S followed by the projection, which yields two tuples: $(1, 2)$ and $(1, \bot')$; the second step eliminates the tuple containing $\bot'$.

Thus, in order to compute the certain answers to a union of conjunctive queries Q with respect to a source instance S, one can use the following procedure. Recall that $\mathcal{M}$ is a mapping such that Σ_t consists of a set of egds and a weakly acyclic set of tgds, and let Q be a union of conjunctive queries.

Algorithm 2 COMPUTECERTAINANSWERS(Q,$\mathcal{M}$)

Require: A source instance S
Ensure: If $\mathrm{SOL}_{\mathcal{M}}(S) \neq \emptyset$, then CA is the set of certain answers for Q over S under $\mathcal{M}$. Otherwise, $CA = \mathtt{fail}$
  1: let T be the result of the chase of S under $\mathcal{M}$
  2: **if** $T = \mathtt{fail}$ **then**
  3:    $CA := \mathtt{fail}$
  4: **else**
  5:    $CA := Q_{\downarrow}(T)$
  6: **end if**

The previous observations imply that

$$certain_{\mathcal{M}}(Q, S) \; = \; Q_{\downarrow}(T). \tag{2.1}$$

In fact, since Q is a union of conjunctive queries, T can be taken to be *any* universal solution, and (2.1) remains true. In particular, if in the above algorithm we compute the core instead of the canonical universal solution, the output of the algorithm is still the set of certain answers.

There is a natural question that arises at this point: What happens if we extend conjunctive queries with a restricted form of negation, e.g., inequalities? Unfortunately, even this slight extension of the language leads to intractability of the problem of computing certain answers, as the next theorem shows.

Theorem 2.25

1. *Let $\mathcal{M}$ be a mapping such that Σ_t consists of a set of egds and a weakly acyclic set of tgds, and let Q be a conjunctive query with inequalities. The problem of computing certain answers for Q and $\mathcal{M}$ is in* coNP.

2. *There is a Boolean conjunctive query Q with inequalities and a LAV mapping $\mathcal{M}$, such that the problem of computing certain answers for Q and $\mathcal{M}$ is* coNP-hard.

Proof. We first prove (1). We show that if there is a solution T for a source instance S such that $\bar{t} \notin Q(T)$, then there is a solution T' of polynomial size such that $\bar{t} \notin Q(T')$. Suppose that T is a solution for S such that $\bar{t} \notin Q(T)$. Let T_{can} be the canonical universal solution for S. (Notice that T_{can} exists since S has at least one solution). Then there is a homomorphism $h : T_{can} \to T$. We denote by $h(T_{can})$ the homomorphic image of T under h (notice that $h(T_{can})$ is a solution for S). We claim that $\bar{t} \notin Q(h(T_{can}))$. Assume otherwise; then $\bar{t} \in Q(h(T_{can}))$. But $h(T_{can})$ is a sub-instance of T, and clearly conjunctive queries with inequalities are preserved under sub-instances. We conclude that $\bar{t} \in Q(T)$, which is a contradiction. Further, notice that T_{can} is of polynomial size, and, thus, $h(T_{can})$ is also a polynomial size.

With this observation, it is easy to construct a coNP algorithm for the problem of certain answers of Q and $\mathcal{M}$. In fact, a coNP algorithm for checking $\bar{t} \in certain_{\mathcal{M}}(Q, S)$ is the same as an NP algorithm for checking $\bar{t} \notin certain_{\mathcal{M}}(Q, S)$. By the above observation, for the latter, it simply suffices to guess a polynomial size instance T and check, in polynomial time, that T is a solution, and that $\bar{t} \notin Q(T)$.

We now prove (2). The LAV mapping $\mathcal{M} = (\mathbf{R_s}, \mathbf{R_t}, \Sigma_{st})$ is as follows. The source schema $\mathbf{R_s}$ consists of two relations: A binary relation P and a ternary relation R. The target schema $\mathbf{R_t}$ also consists of two relations: A binary relation U and a ternary relation V. Further, Σ_{st} is the following set of source-to-target dependencies:

$$
\begin{aligned}
P(x, y) \;&\to\; \exists z (U(x, z) \land U(y, z)) \\
R(x, y, z) \;&\to\; V(x, y, z)
\end{aligned}
$$

The Boolean query Q is defined as:

$$\exists x_1 \exists y_1 \exists x_2 \exists y_2 \exists x_3 \exists y_3 (V(x_1, x_2, x_3) \wedge U(x_1, y_1) \wedge$$
$$U(x_2, y_2) \wedge U(x_3, y_3) \wedge x_1 \neq y_1 \wedge x_2 \neq y_2 \wedge x_3 \neq y_3).$$

Next, we show that the problem of certain answers for Q and $\mathcal{M}$ is coNP-hard.

The coNP-hardness is established from a reduction from 3SAT to the complement of the problem of certain answers for Q and $\mathcal{M}$. More precisely, for every 3CNF propositional formula φ, we construct in polynomial time an instance S_φ of $\mathbf{R_s}$ such that φ is satisfiable iff $certain_\mathcal{M}(Q, S_\varphi) =$ false.

Given a propositional formula $\varphi \equiv \bigwedge_{1 \le j \le m} C_j$ in 3CNF, where each C_j is a clause, let S_φ be the following source instance:

- The interpretation of P in S_φ contains the pair $(q, \neg q)$, for each propositional variable q mentioned in φ; and

- the interpretation of R in S_φ contains all tuples (α, β, γ) such that for some $j \in \{1, \ldots, m\}$, $C_j = (\alpha \vee \beta \vee \gamma)$.

Clearly, S_φ can be constructed in polynomial time from φ.

It is not hard to see that the canonical universal solution T for S_φ is as follows, where we denote by $\perp_q$ the null generated by applying the st-tgd $P(x, y) \to \exists z(U(x, z) \wedge U(y, z))$ to $P(q, \neg q)$:

- The interpretation of the relation U in T contains the tuples $(q, \perp_q)$ and $(\neg q, \perp_q)$, for each propositional variable q mentioned in φ; and

- the interpretation of the relation V in T is just a copy of the interpretation of the relation R in S_φ.

We leave as an exercise to the reader to prove that φ is satisfiable iff $certain_\mathcal{M}(Q, S_\varphi) =$ false. This finishes the proof of the theorem. $\square$

2.4.2 QUERY REWRITING

As we have seen, a desirable property for query answering in data exchange is being able to compute the certain answers to a query Q using a materialized solution. But notice that the query one evaluates over such a materialized solution is not necessarily the original query Q but rather a query obtained from Q, or, in other words, a *rewriting* of Q. The key property of such a rewriting Q' is that, for each given source S and materialized target T, we have

$$certain_\mathcal{M}(Q, S) = Q'(T). \tag{2.2}$$

Comparing this with (2.1), we see that $Q_\downarrow$ was a rewriting for unions of conjunctive queries, over universal solutions.

In general, the rewriting Q' of a query Q need not be a query in the same language as Q. But usually, one looks for rewritings in languages with polynomial time data complexity (e.g., FO). In this chapter, we deal with FO rewritings.

We now define the notion of rewritings precisely. For that, we shall use a unary predicate $\mathbf{C}$ that distinguishes constants in target instances. The extension of the target schema $\mathbf{R_t}$ with this predicate $\mathbf{C}$ is denoted by $\mathbf{R_t^C}$. For the rest of this section, we only deal with mappings without target dependencies (in particular, for avoiding the problem of the existence of universal solutions).

Definition 2.26 (Rewritings).   Assume that $\mathcal{L}$ is a query language. Let $\mathcal{M}$ be a mapping without target dependencies and let Q be a query over the target schema $\mathbf{R_t}$. We say that Q is FO-*rewritable over the canonical universal solution (resp. the core) under* $\mathcal{M}$, if there is a FO-query Q' over $\mathbf{R_t^C}$ such that $certain_\mathcal{M}(Q, S) = Q'(T)$, for every source instance S with canonical universal solution (resp. core) T.   □

The following facts are known about rewritings in data exchange. The first two follow from what we have already mentioned.

- Unions of conjunctive queries are FO-rewritable under any mapping $\mathcal{M}$ without target dependencies, both over the canonical universal solution and the core. Indeed, we have seen that the rewriting of a union of conjunctive queries $Q(x_1, \ldots, x_m)$ is the query $Q_\downarrow$, which is obtained by evaluating Q and only keeping tuples without nulls. It can therefore be expressed as

$$Q(x_1, \ldots, x_m) \wedge \mathbf{C}(x_1) \wedge \cdots \wedge \mathbf{C}(x_m).$$

  Notice that this rewriting is a union of conjunctive queries as well, is independent of the mapping, and can be constructed in polynomial time from $Q(x_1, \ldots, x_m)$.

- There exists a Boolean conjunctive query Q with a single inequality and a LAV mapping $\mathcal{M}$, such that Q is not FO-rewritable under $\mathcal{M}$, both over the canonical universal solution and over the core.

- It is undecidable whether an FO query admits an FO-rewriting over the canonical universal solution or the core. This follows easily from Trakhtenbrot's theorem.

What is the relationship between rewritability over the canonical universal solution and over the core? The following result gives a precise answer to this question.

Theorem 2.27   *For mappings without target constraints Σ_t, the following hold:*

1. *Every* FO *query Q that is* FO-*rewritable over the core is also rewritable over the canonical universal solution.*

2. *There is a mapping $\mathcal{M}$ and an* FO *query Q that is* FO-*rewritable over the canonical universal solution but not over the core.*

Thus, there is the following tradeoff in choosing the canonical universal solution or the core as the preferred solution in data exchange:

- the core allows the most compact materialization among all possible universal solutions; however,

- this comes at the cost of losing the capability for FO-rewriting of some queries.

2.5   SUMMARY

- Without putting restrictions on schema mappings, all the key computational tasks are undecidable in data exchange. Hence, one usually deals with the mappings in which:

  1. the relationship between the source and the target schemas is specified by source-to-target tuple generating dependencies (st-tgds), and
  2. the target constraints are tuple-generating and equality-generating dependencies (tgds and egds).

- Even in this setting, the problem of checking whether a given source admits a solution is undecidable. Hence, one usually imposes a further acyclicity condition on the target constraints.

- With this condition (called weak acyclicity), solutions – if they exist – can be constructed in polynomial time by the chase procedure. If the chase fails, it means that there are no solutions.

- Solutions constructed by the chase are more general than others – they are so-called universal solutions. There are several equivalent ways of stating that a solution is more general than others. The result of the chase is usually referred to as the canonical universal solution.

- Certain answers for an arbitrary conjunctive query Q (or unions of conjunctive queries) can be found if one has an arbitrary universal solution: this is done by means of answering another query, the rewriting of Q, over the solution.

- There is a unique minimal universal solution, called the core. It can be constructed in polynomial time under the weak acyclicity assumption, although the algorithm is quite complicated. A simpler algorithm exists if target constraints contain only egds.

- Any relational calculus query that is rewritable over the core is rewritable over the canonical universal solution, but not vice versa.

2.6   BIBLIOGRAPHICAL COMMENTS

The basics of data exchange were described by Fagin et al. [2005a]. That paper presented the notion of schema mappings as we use them, adapted the chase procedure to the data exchange setting, and introduced universal solutions (using the definition based on homomorphisms). The central notion of weak acyclicity was first formulated by Deutsch and Popa, and later independently used by Fagin et al. [2005a], and Deutsch and Tannen [2003]. Given the role of chase in data exchange, finding conditions for its termination is an active research topic. Recent results show that chase can be pushed beyond weak acyclicity [Deutsch et al., 2008; Marnette, 2009; Meier et al., 2009]. Complexity of the key tasks associated with data exchange was studied by Kolaitis et al. [2006], who also studied the combined complexity of checking for the existence of solutions (i.e., the complexity of the problem when the mapping itself is considered to be part of the input).

The notion of core originates in graph theory [P. Hell and J. Nešetřil, 2004]. Its usefulness in data exchange was shown by Fagin et al. [2005b], who gave the simple algorithm for computing cores. The polynomial-time algorithm for the general case was developed by Gottlob and Nash [2008].

The algorithm for answering conjunctive queries based on naive evaluation [Imielinski and Lipski, 1984] was given by Fagin et al. [2005a]. While extension of this algorithm to full FO is impossible, some limited form of negation can be used in queries [Arenas et al., 2009a]. The notions of rewritings over the core and the canonical universal solution were studied by Fagin et al. [2005a,b]; the result showing the exact relationship between them is by Arenas et al. [2004].

It was also shown by Arenas et al. [2004] that query answering in data exchange may exhibit unnatural behavior. It was argued by Libkin [2006] that this is due to the openness of solutions to adding new facts. A different semantics for data exchange based on *closed* world assumption was proposed [Libkin, 2006] and shown to avoid some of the unwanted behavior noticed by Arenas et al. [2004]; further extensions were given by Hernich and Schweikardt [2007], Libkin and Sirangelo [2008], and Afrati and Kolaitis [2008], who considered aggregate queries in a data exchange scenario.

An approach to justifying classes of mappings based on their structural properties was developed by ten Cate and Kolaitis [2009]. An extension of schema mappings that works in a bi-directional way was given by Fuxman et al. [2006].

CHAPTER 3

Metadata Management

3.1 INTRODUCTION

In the last few years, a lot of attention has been paid to the development of solid foundations for the problem of exchanging data using schema mappings. These developments are a first step towards providing a general framework for exchanging information, but they are definitely not the last one. As pointed out in the literature, many information system problems involve not only the design and integration of complex application artifacts, but also their subsequent manipulation. This has motivated the need for the development of a general infrastructure for managing schema mappings.

A schema mapping is a specification that describes how data from a source schema is to be mapped to a target schema. As such, a schema mapping provides *metadata*. Thus, the problem of managing schema mappings has been called *metadata management* in the literature.

A metadata management framework, called model management, has been recently proposed. In this framework, mappings are usually specified in a logical language, and high-level algebraic operators such as match, merge, compose and invert are used to manipulate them. For instance, next we show the intuition behind the composition operator, and show how it can be used in practice to solve some metadata management problems. Let $\mathcal{M}_{12}$ be the mapping given in Chapter 1, which is used to translate information from a source schema $\mathbf{R_1}$, consisting of relations GEO(city, country, population) and FLIGHT(source, destination, airline, departure), into a target schema $\mathbf{R_2}$, consisting of relations ROUTES(flight#, source, destination), INFO_FLIGHT(flight#, departure_time, arrival_time, airline) and SERVES(airline, city, country, phone). Mapping $\mathcal{M}_{12}$ is specified by using the logical language of source-to-target tuple-generating dependencies (st-tgds):

FLIGHT(src, dest, airl, dep) $\longrightarrow$
$\qquad \exists$f# $\exists$arr (ROUTES(f#, src, dest) $\wedge$ INFO_FLIGHT(f#, dep, arr, airl))
FLIGHT(city, dest, airl, dep) $\wedge$ GEO(city, country, popul) $\longrightarrow$
$\qquad \exists$phone SERVES(airl, city, country, phone)
FLIGHT(src, city, airl, dep) $\wedge$ GEO(city, country, popul) $\longrightarrow$
$\qquad \exists$phone SERVES(airl, city, country, phone)

Assume that schema $\mathbf{R_2}$ has to be updated into a new target schema $\mathbf{R_3}$ consisting of the following relations:

- INFO_AIRLINE(airline, city, country, phone, year)

INFO_AIRLINE has information about cities served by airlines: for example, it may have a tuple (AirFrance, Santiago, Chile, 5550000, 1982), indicating that AirFrance serves Santiago, Chile, since 1982, and its office there can be reached at 555-0000.

- INFO_JOURNEY(flight#, source, departure_time, destination, arrival_time, airline)

   This relation has information about routes served by several airlines. For each flight, this relation stores the flight number (flight#), source, departure time, destination, arrival time and the name of the airline.

Furthermore, assume that the relationship between R_2 and the new target schema R_3 is given by a mapping $\mathcal{M}_{23}$, which is specified by the following source-to-target dependencies:

SERVES(airl, city, country, phone) $\longrightarrow$
$\qquad\qquad$ ∃year INFO_AIRLINE(airl, city, country, phone, year)
ROUTES(f#, src, dest) ∧ INFO_FLIGHT(f#, dep, arr, airl) $\longrightarrow$
$\qquad\qquad$ INFO_JOURNEY(f#, src, dep, dest, arr, airl)

Given that R_2 has to be replaced by the new target schema R_3, the mapping $\mathcal{M}_{12}$ from schema R_1 into schema R_2 also has to be replaced by a new mapping $\mathcal{M}_{13}$, which specifies how to translate data from R_1 into the new target schema R_3. Thus, the problem in this scenario is to compute a new mapping $\mathcal{M}_{13}$ that represents the application of mapping $\mathcal{M}_{12}$ followed by the application of mapping $\mathcal{M}_{23}$. But given that mappings are binary relations from a semantic point of view, this problem corresponds to the computation of the composition of mappings $\mathcal{M}_{12}$ and $\mathcal{M}_{23}$. In fact, the composition operator for schema mappings exactly computes this, and in this particular example, returns a mapping $\mathcal{M}_{13}$ specified by the following source-to-target dependencies:

FLIGHT(src, dest, airl, dep) $\longrightarrow$
$\qquad\qquad$ ∃f# ∃arr INFO_JOURNEY(f#, src, dep, dest, arr, airl)
FLIGHT(city, dest, airl, dep) ∧ GEO(city, country, popul) $\longrightarrow$
$\qquad\qquad$ ∃phone ∃year INFO_AIRLINE(airl, city, country, phone, year)
FLIGHT(src, city, airl, dep) ∧ GEO(city, country, popul) $\longrightarrow$
$\qquad\qquad$ ∃phone ∃year INFO_AIRLINE(airl, city, country, phone, year)

In this chapter, we study two of the operators that have been identified as crucial for the development of a metadata management framework, namely the *composition* and *inverse* operators. Specifically, we concentrate on the following issues for each of these notions: the definition of its semantics, the study of the language needed to express it and the algorithmic issues associated to the problem of computing it.

3.2   COMPOSITION OF SCHEMA MAPPINGS

The composition operator has been identified as one of the fundamental operators for the development of a framework for managing schema mappings. The goal of this operator is to generate a mapping $\mathcal{M}_{13}$ that has the same effect as applying successively two given mappings $\mathcal{M}_{12}$ and $\mathcal{M}_{23}$, provided that the target schema of $\mathcal{M}_{12}$ is the same as the source schema of $\mathcal{M}_{23}$.

As mentioned in the introduction, the semantics of the composition operator can be defined in terms of the semantics of this operator for binary relations.

Definition 3.1   (Composition operator).   Let $\mathcal{M}_{12}$ be a mapping from a schema $\mathbf{R_1}$ to a schema $\mathbf{R_2}$, and $\mathcal{M}_{23}$ a mapping from $\mathbf{R_2}$ to a schema $\mathbf{R_3}$. Then the composition of $\mathcal{M}_{12}$ and $\mathcal{M}_{23}$ is defined as

$$\mathcal{M}_{12} \circ \mathcal{M}_{23} \;\; = \;\; \{(S_1, S_3) \mid \exists S_2 : (S_1, S_2) \in \mathcal{M}_{12} \text{ and } (S_2, S_3) \in \mathcal{M}_{23}\}.$$

To reduce the clutter, we shall often write $(S, T) \in \mathcal{M}$ instead of the more formal $(S, T) \in [\![\mathcal{M}]\!]$.

For the mappings $\mathcal{M}_{12}$, $\mathcal{M}_{23}$ and $\mathcal{M}_{13}$ shown in the introduction of this chapter, $\mathcal{M}_{13}$ corresponds to the composition of $\mathcal{M}_{12}$ and $\mathcal{M}_{23}$ since $[\![\mathcal{M}_{13}]\!] = [\![\mathcal{M}_{12} \circ \mathcal{M}_{23}]\!]$. It is important to notice that this example shows two mappings specified by st-tgds, whose composition can also be specified by these dependencies. This motivates the first fundamental question about the composition operator, namely, whether the composition of st-tgds can always be specified in the same logical language. At a first glance, one may be tempted to think that the answer to this question is positive, and that the example in the introduction can be generalized to any composition of st-tgds. However, the following example proves that this is not the case, as it shows two mappings specified by st-tgds whose composition cannot be specified by a set of these dependencies.

Example 3.2   Consider a schema $\mathbf{R_1}$ consisting of one binary relation Takes, that associates a student name with a course she/he is taking, a schema $\mathbf{R_2}$ consisting of a relation Takes_1, that is intended to be a copy of Takes, and of an additional relation symbol Student, that associates a student with a student id; and a schema $\mathbf{R_3}$ consisting of a binary relation symbol Enrollment, that associates a student id with the courses this student is taking. Consider now mappings $\mathcal{M}_{12}$ and $\mathcal{M}_{23}$ specified by the following sets of st-tgds:

$$\Sigma_{12} \;\; = \;\; \{\text{Takes}(n, c) \to \text{Takes}_1(n, c), \quad \text{Takes}(n, c) \to \exists s\, \text{Student}(n, s)\},$$
$$\Sigma_{23} \;\; = \;\; \{\text{Student}(n, s) \wedge \text{Takes}_1(n, c) \to \text{Enrollment}(s, c)\}.$$

Mapping $\mathcal{M}_{12}$ requires that a copy of every tuple in Takes must exist in Takes_1 and, moreover, that each student name n must be associated with some student id s in the relation Student. Mapping $\mathcal{M}_{23}$ requires that if a student with name n and id s takes a course c, then (s, c) is a tuple in the relation Enrollment. Intuitively, in the composition mapping, one would like to replace the name

n of a student by a student id i_n, and then for each course c that is taken by n, one would like to include the tuple (i_n, c) in the table Enrollment. Unfortunately, it can be formally proved that it is not possible to express this relationship by using a set of st-tgds. In particular, a st-tgd of the form:

$$\text{Takes}(n, c) \quad \rightarrow \quad \exists y \, \text{Enrollment}(y, c) \tag{3.1}$$

does not express the desired relationship, as it may associate a distinct student id y for each tuple (n, c) in Takes and, thus, it may create several identifiers for the same student name. □

The previous example shows that in order to express the composition of mappings specified by st-tgds, one has to use a language more expressive than st-tgds. However, the example gives little information about what the right language for composition is. In fact, the composition of mappings $\mathcal{M}_{12}$ and $\mathcal{M}_{23}$ in this example can be defined in first-order logic:

$$\forall n \exists y \forall c \, (\text{Takes}(n, c) \rightarrow \text{Enrollment}(y, c)),$$

which may lead to the conclusion that FO is a good alternative to define the composition of mappings specified by st-tgds. However, a complexity argument shows that this conclusion is incorrect. More specifically, given mappings $\mathcal{M}_{12} = (\mathbf{R_1}, \mathbf{R_2}, \Sigma_{12})$ and $\mathcal{M}_{23} = (\mathbf{R_2}, \mathbf{R_3}, \Sigma_{23})$, where Σ_{12} and Σ_{23} are sets of st-tgds, define the *composition problem for $\mathcal{M}_{12}$ and $\mathcal{M}_{23}$*, denoted by COMPOSITION($\mathcal{M}_{12}, \mathcal{M}_{23}$), as the problem of verifying, given $S_1 \in \text{INST}(\mathbf{R_1})$ and $S_3 \in \text{INST}(\mathbf{R_3})$, whether $(S_1, S_3) \in \mathcal{M}_{12} \circ \mathcal{M}_{23}$. If the composition of $\mathcal{M}_{12}$ with $\mathcal{M}_{23}$ is defined by a finite set Σ of formulas in some logical formalism, then COMPOSITION($\mathcal{M}_{12}, \mathcal{M}_{23}$) is reduced to the problem of verifying whether a pair of instances (S_1, S_3) satisfies Σ. In particular, if Σ is a set of FO formulas, then the complexity of COMPOSITION($\mathcal{M}_{12}, \mathcal{M}_{23}$) is in AC^0, as the complexity of the problem of verifying whether a fixed set of FO formulas is satisfied by an instance is in this complexity class [1]. Thus, if the complexity of COMPOSITION($\mathcal{M}_{12}, \mathcal{M}_{23}$) is higher than AC^0, for some mappings $\mathcal{M}_{12}$ and $\mathcal{M}_{23}$ specified by st-tgds, then one can conclude that the composition cannot be expressed in FO. In fact, the following theorem shows that the latter holds, as the complexity of COMPOSITION($\mathcal{M}_{12}, \mathcal{M}_{23}$) can be NP-complete, and it is well-known that $\text{AC}^0 \subsetneq \text{NP}$.

Theorem 3.3 *For every pair of mappings $\mathcal{M}_{12}, \mathcal{M}_{23}$ specified by st-tgds, COMPOSITION($\mathcal{M}_{12}, \mathcal{M}_{23}$) is in NP. Moreover, there exist mappings $\mathcal{M}_{12}^\star$ and $\mathcal{M}_{23}^\star$ specified by st-tgds such that COMPOSITION($\mathcal{M}_{12}^\star, \mathcal{M}_{23}^\star$) is NP-complete.*

Proof. The membership of COMPOSITION($\mathcal{M}_{12}, \mathcal{M}_{23}$) in NP can be proved by showing that there exists a polynomial p (that depends on $\mathcal{M}_{12}$ and $\mathcal{M}_{23}$) such that if $(S_1, S_3) \in \mathcal{M}_{12} \circ \mathcal{M}_{23}$, then there exists an instance S_2 satisfying that $(S_1, S_2) \in \mathcal{M}_{12}$, $(S_2, S_3) \in \mathcal{M}_{23}$ and $\|S_2\| \leq p(\|S_1\| + \|S_3\|)$.

---

[1]Recall that AC^0 is the class of problems that can be accepted by a family of constant-depth, unbounded-fanin circuits with AND, OR, and NOT gates. Its uniform version, which contains FO, is a subclass of LOGSPACE, and thus PTIME.

We leave this proof for the reader, and we focus here on showing that COMPOSITION($\mathcal{M}_{12}$, $\mathcal{M}_{23}$) can be NP-hard.

Let $\mathbf{R_1}$ be a schema consisting of a unary relation node and a binary relation edge, $\mathbf{R_2}$ a schema consisting of binary relations coloring and edge', and $\mathbf{R_3}$ a schema consisting of a binary relation error and a unary relation color. Moreover, let $\mathcal{M}_{12}^\star = (\mathbf{R_1}, \mathbf{R_2}, \Sigma_{12})$ and $\mathcal{M}_{23}^\star = (\mathbf{R_2}, \mathbf{R_3}, \Sigma_{23})$, where Σ_{12} consists of the following st-tgds:

$$\begin{aligned} \text{node}(x) &\rightarrow \exists y\, \text{coloring}(x, y), \\ \text{edge}(x, y) &\rightarrow \text{edge}'(x, y), \end{aligned} \tag{3.2}$$

and Σ_{23} consists of the following st-tgds:

$$\begin{aligned} \text{edge}'(x, y) \wedge \text{coloring}(x, u) \wedge \text{coloring}(y, u) &\rightarrow \text{error}(x, y), &&(3.3) \\ \text{coloring}(x, y) &\rightarrow \text{color}(y). &&(3.4) \end{aligned}$$

Next, we show that COMPOSITION($\mathcal{M}_{12}^\star$, $\mathcal{M}_{23}^\star$) is NP-hard by reducing from the graph 3-coloring problem. Intuitively, relations node and edge in $\mathbf{R_1}$ store a graph G, and relation edge' in $\mathbf{R_2}$ is a copy of edge. Moreover, st-tgd (3.2) indicates that a color must be assigned to each node in the graph and, thus, relation coloring in $\mathbf{R_2}$ stores a possible coloring of graph G. Finally, st-tgd (3.4) indicates that relation color in $\mathbf{R_3}$ stores the colors used in the coloring of G, and st-tgd (3.3) indicates that error stores any incorrect assignment of colors, that is, error(x, y) holds if x, y are adjacent nodes in G and the same color is assigned to them.

Formally, let $G = (N, E)$ be a graph, and define instances S_1 of $\mathbf{R_1}$ and S_3 of $\mathbf{R_3}$ as follows:

$$\begin{aligned} \text{node}^{S_1} &= N, & \text{color}^{S_3} &= \{red,\ green,\ blue\}, \\ \text{edge}^{S_1} &= E, & \text{error}^{S_3} &= \emptyset. \end{aligned}$$

Then, it holds that $(S_1, S_3) \in \mathcal{M}_{12}^\star \circ \mathcal{M}_{23}^\star$, if and only if graph G is 3-colorable. This concludes the proof of the theorem, as it shows that the graph 3-coloring problem can be reduced in polynomial time to COMPOSITION($\mathcal{M}_{12}^\star$, $\mathcal{M}_{23}^\star$). $\square$

Theorem 3.3 not only shows that FO is not the right language to express the composition of mappings given by st-tgds but also gives a good insight on what needs to be added to st-tgds to obtain a language capable of expressing the composition of these dependencies. Given that COMPOSITION($\mathcal{M}_{12}$, $\mathcal{M}_{23}$) is in NP, one concludes from Fagin's Theorem that the composition can be defined by an existential second-order logic formula. In fact, it is shown in the following section that the extension of st-tgds with existential second-order quantification gives rise to the *right* mapping language for dealing with the composition operator.

3.2.1   EXTENDING ST-TGDS WITH SECOND-ORDER QUANTIFICATION

In the previous section, we showed that FO is not expressive enough to represent the composition of mappings given by st-tgds, and that the existential fragment of second-order logic can be used to express the composition of this type of mappings. In this section, we go deeper into this, and we show that the extension of st-tgds with existential second-order quantification is the right language for composition.

Formally, given schemas $\mathbf{R_s}$ and $\mathbf{R_t}$ with no relation symbols in common, a *second-order tuple-generating dependency from* $\mathbf{R_s}$ *to* $\mathbf{R_t}$ (SO tgd) is a formula of the form:

$$\exists f_1 \cdots \exists f_m \left(\forall \bar{x}_1 (\varphi_1 \rightarrow \psi_1) \wedge \cdots \wedge \forall \bar{x}_n (\varphi_n \rightarrow \psi_n) \right),$$

where

1. each f_i $(1 \leq i \leq m)$ is a function symbol,

2. each formula φ_i $(1 \leq i \leq n)$ is a conjunction of relational atoms of the form $P(y_1, \ldots, y_k)$ and equality atoms of the form $t = t'$, where P is a k-ary relation symbol of $\mathbf{R_s}$ and $y_1, \ldots, y_k$ are (not necessarily distinct) variables in $\bar{x}_i$, and t, t' are terms built from $\bar{x}_i$ and $f_1, \ldots, f_m$,

3. each formula ψ_i $(1 \leq i \leq n)$ is a conjunction of relational atomic formulas of the form $R(t_1, \ldots, t_\ell)$, where R is an ℓ-ary relation symbol of $\mathbf{R_t}$ and $t_1, \ldots t_\ell$ are terms built from $\bar{x}_i$ and $f_1, \ldots, f_m$, and

4. each variable in $\bar{x}_i$ $(1 \leq i \leq n)$ appears in some relational atom of φ_i.

To define the semantics of SO tgds, it is necessary to specify the semantics of the existential second-order quantifiers in these dependencies. In particular, in deciding whether $(S, T) \models \sigma$, for an SO tgd σ, what should the domain and range of the functions instantiating the existentially quantified function symbols be? The obvious choice is to let the domain and range be the domain of (S, T), but it has been shown in the data exchange literature that this does not work properly. Instead, the semantics of SO tgds is defined as follows. Let σ be an SO tgd from a schema $\mathbf{R_s}$ to a schema $\mathbf{R_t}$, and assume that S is an instance of $\mathbf{R_s}$ and T is an instance of $\mathbf{R_t}$. Then (S, T) satisfies σ, denoted by $(S, T) \models \sigma$, if $\mathfrak{A}_{(S,T)} \models \sigma$ under the standard notion of satisfaction in second-order logic, where $\mathfrak{A}_{(S,T)}$ is a structure obtained from (S, T) as follows. The domain of $\mathfrak{A}_{(S,T)}$ is $\mathtt{Const} \cup \mathtt{Var}$. Moreover, for every relation P in $\mathbf{R_s}$, the interpretation of P in $\mathfrak{A}_{(S,T)}$ is P^S, and for every relation R in $\mathbf{R_t}$, the interpretation of R in $\mathfrak{A}_{(S,T)}$ is R^T.

Example 3.4   Let $\mathbf{R_s}$ be a source schema consisting of a unary relation P, $\mathbf{R_t}$ a target schema consisting of a unary relation R, and σ the following SO tgd from $\mathbf{R_s}$ to $\mathbf{R_t}$:

$$\exists f \left(\forall x \, (P(x) \wedge x = f(x) \rightarrow R(x)) \right).$$

Let S be an instance of $\mathbf{R_s}$ defined as $P^S = \{a\}$, and assume that T is the empty instance of $\mathbf{R_t}$. According to the above definition, $(S, T) \models \sigma$ since $\mathfrak{A}_{(S,T)} \models \sigma$ with any interpretation of f that maps a to an element b such that $a \neq b$. On the other hand, if one is not allowed to include extra values in deciding whether (S, T) satisfies σ, then $(S, T) \not\models \sigma$, as in this case, the only possible interpretation of f maps a into itself since $\text{Dom}(S) \cup \text{Dom}(T) = \{a\}$. $\qquad\qquad\square$

As shown in the previous example, the inclusion of extra values when interpreting the function symbols of an SO tgd makes a difference. But it should be noticed that the possibility of using an infinite set of extra values is not significant in the case of SO tgd, as instead of taking the domain of $\mathfrak{A}_{(S,T)}$ to be $(\text{Const} \cup \text{Var})$, one can take it to be finite and sufficiently large:

Proposition 3.5   *Let σ be an SO tgd from a schema $\mathbf{R_s}$ to a schema $\mathbf{R_t}$. Then there exists a polynomial p, which depends only on σ, with the following property. Assume that S is an instance of $\mathbf{R_s}$, T is an instance of $\mathbf{R_t}$, U is a set such that $(\text{Dom}(S) \cup \text{Dom}(T)) \subseteq U \subseteq (\text{Const} \cup \text{Var})$ and $|U| \geq p(\|S\| + \|T\|)$, and $\mathfrak{A}^U_{(S,T)}$ is defined as $\mathfrak{A}_{(S,T)}$, except that it has domain U. Then $\mathfrak{A}_{(S,T)} \models \sigma$ if and only if $\mathfrak{A}^U_{(S,T)} \models \sigma$.*

Several features of SO tgds make them the right language for composition. First, it is not difficult to prove that every set of st-tgds can be transformed into an SO tgd. In fact, the well-known Skolemization method can be used to compute an SO tgd equivalent to a set of st-tgds. For example, the following set of st-tgds from Example 3.2:

$$\{\text{Takes}(n, c) \rightarrow \text{Takes}_1(n, c), \ \text{Takes}(n, c) \rightarrow \exists s \, \text{Student}(n, s)\}$$

is equivalent to SO tgd:

$$\exists f \Big(\forall n \forall c \, (\text{Takes}(n, c) \rightarrow \text{Takes}_1(n, c)) \ \wedge \ \forall n \forall c \, (\text{Takes}(n, c) \rightarrow \text{Student}(n, f(n, c))) \Big).$$

Second, it is possible to prove that SO tgds are closed under composition. That is, given an SO tgd σ_{12} from a schema $\mathbf{R_1}$ to a schema $\mathbf{R_2}$, and an SO tgd σ_{23} from $\mathbf{R_2}$ to a schema $\mathbf{R_3}$, there exists an SO tgd σ_{13} from $\mathbf{R_1}$ to $\mathbf{R_3}$ such that $\mathcal{M}_{13} = \mathcal{M}_{12} \circ \mathcal{M}_{23}$, where $\mathcal{M}_{13}$, $\mathcal{M}_{12}$ and $\mathcal{M}_{23}$ are the mappings defined by σ_{13}, σ_{12} and σ_{23}, respectively.

Example 3.6   We show here how to compute the composition of two SO tgds by considering a variation of the mappings used in the proof of Theorem 3.3. Let $\mathbf{R_1}$ be a schema consisting of a unary relation node and a binary relation edge, $\mathbf{R_2}$ a schema consisting of binary relations coloring and edge', and $\mathbf{R_3}$ a schema consisting of unary relations error and color. Moreover, let $\mathcal{M}_{12} = (\mathbf{R_1}, \mathbf{R_2}, \Sigma_{12})$ and $\mathcal{M}_{23} = (\mathbf{R_2}, \mathbf{R_3}, \Sigma_{23})$, where Σ_{12} consists of the following st-tgds:

$$\begin{aligned} \text{node}(x) &\rightarrow \exists y \, \text{coloring}(x, y), \\ \text{edge}(x, y) &\rightarrow \text{edge}'(x, y), \end{aligned}$$

and Σ_{23} consists of the following st-tgds:

$$\begin{aligned} \text{edge}'(x, y) \wedge \text{coloring}(x, u) \wedge \text{coloring}(y, u) &\rightarrow \exists v \, \text{error}(v), \\ \text{coloring}(x, y) &\rightarrow \text{color}(y). \end{aligned}$$

As in the proof of Theorem 3.3, it is possible to prove that the composition of $\mathcal{M}_{12}$ and $\mathcal{M}_{23}$ can be used to encode the graph 3-coloring problem.

Consider now the SO tgds representing mappings $\mathcal{M}_{12}$ and $\mathcal{M}_{23}$. That is, let σ_{12} be the following SO tgd:

$$\exists f \left(\forall x \, (\texttt{node}(x) \rightarrow \texttt{coloring}(x, f(x))) \wedge \forall x \forall y \, (\texttt{edge}(x, y) \rightarrow \texttt{edge}'(x, y)) \right),$$

which is equivalent to Σ_{12}, and let σ_{23} be the following SO tgd:

$$\exists g \left(\forall x \forall y \forall u \, (\texttt{edge}'(x, y) \wedge \texttt{coloring}(x, u) \wedge \texttt{coloring}(y, u) \rightarrow \texttt{error}(g(x, y, u))) \wedge \right.$$
$$\left. \forall x \forall y \, (\texttt{coloring}(x, y) \rightarrow \texttt{color}(y)) \right),$$

which is equivalent to Σ_{23}. Next we show the essential steps of an algorithm that constructs an SO tgd σ_{13} defining the composition of the mappings specified by σ_{12} and σ_{23}. As a first step, for every conjunct $\forall \bar{x} \, (\varphi \rightarrow \psi)$ of σ_{12}, each non-atomic term t in ψ is eliminated by replacing it by a fresh variable u and including equality $u = t$ in φ. More specifically, σ_{12} is replaced by the following dependency:

$$\exists f \left(\forall x \forall y \, (\texttt{node}(x) \wedge y = f(x) \rightarrow \texttt{coloring}(x, y)) \wedge \right.$$
$$\left. \forall x \forall y \, (\texttt{edge}(x, y) \rightarrow \texttt{edge}'(x, y)) \right). \quad (3.5)$$

It is important to notice that (3.5) is not an SO tgd as it does not satisfy condition (4) in the definition of SO tgds (variable y in the first conjunct of (3.5) is mentioned neither in predicate node nor in predicate edge). As a second step, the algorithm replaces every relational atom in the premise of a conjunct of σ_{23} by its definition according to (3.5), that is, $\texttt{coloring}(x, y)$ is replaced by $(\texttt{node}(x) \wedge y = f(x))$ and $\texttt{edge}'(x, y)$ is replaced by $\texttt{edge}(x, y)$. The following formula is obtained as a result of this process:

$$\exists f \exists g \left(\forall x \forall y \forall u \, (\texttt{edge}(x, y) \wedge \texttt{node}(x) \wedge u = f(x) \wedge \right.$$
$$\texttt{node}(y) \wedge u = f(y) \rightarrow \texttt{error}(g(x, y, u))) \wedge$$
$$\left. \forall x \forall y \, (\texttt{node}(x) \wedge y = f(x) \rightarrow \texttt{color}(y)) \right). \quad (3.6)$$

Again, it is important to notice that (3.6) is not an SO tgd as it does not satisfy condition (4) in the definition of SO tgds. As a final step, the algorithm transforms (3.6) into an SO tgd by eliminating all the variables that do not satisfy the aforementioned condition (4). This final step is achieved by replacing these variables by the terms that are equal to according to (3.6). More precisely, u is replaced by $f(y)$ in the first conjunct of (3.6), while y is replaced by $f(x)$ in the second conjunct of this formula:

$$\exists f \exists g \left(\forall x \forall y \, (\text{edge}(x, y) \wedge \text{node}(x) \wedge \right.$$
$$\text{node}(y) \wedge f(x) = f(y) \rightarrow \text{error}(g(x, y, f(y)))) \wedge$$
$$\left. \forall x \, (\text{node}(x) \rightarrow \text{color}(f(x))) \right). \quad (3.7)$$

Dependency (3.7) is the SO tgd returned by the algorithm. In fact, it can be proved that (3.7) defines the composition of the mappings specified by σ_{12} and σ_{23}. To see why this is the case, we show how (3.7) can be used to represent the graph 3-coloring problem. It should be noticed that (3.7) is equivalent to the following SO tgd:

$$\exists f \exists h \left(\forall x \forall y \, (\text{edge}(x, y) \wedge \text{node}(x) \wedge \right.$$
$$\text{node}(y) \wedge f(x) = f(y) \rightarrow \text{error}(h(x, y)) \wedge$$
$$\left. \forall x \, (\text{node}(x) \rightarrow \text{color}(f(x))) \right), \quad (3.8)$$

which is obtained by defining function $h(x, y)$ as $g(x, y, f(y))$. Furthermore, relations node and edge in (3.8) store a graph G, $f(a)$ is the color assigned to a node a of G in (3.8), and error stores any incorrect assignment of colors, that is, $\text{error}(h(a, b))$ holds if a, b are adjacent nodes in G and the same color is assigned to them (which corresponds to the condition $f(a) = f(b)$). $\qquad \square$

The following theorem shows that the composition algorithm presented in the previous example can be generalized to any pair of SO tgds.

Theorem 3.7   *Let $\mathcal{M}_{12}$ and $\mathcal{M}_{23}$ be mappings specified by SO tgds. Then the composition $\mathcal{M}_{12} \circ \mathcal{M}_{23}$ can also be specified by an SO tgd.*

It should be noticed that the previous theorem can also be applied to mappings that are specified by finite sets of SO tgds, as these dependencies are closed under conjunction. Moreover, it is important to notice that Theorem 3.7 implies that the composition of a finite number of mappings specified by st-tgds can be defined by an SO tgd, as every set of st-tgds can be expressed as an SO tgd.

Theorem 3.8   *The composition of a finite number of mappings, each defined by a finite set of st-tgds, is defined by an SO tgd.*

Example 3.9   We have already shown in Example 3.6 how SO tgds can be used to express the composition of mappings specified by st-tgds. As a second example, assume that $\mathcal{M}_{12}$ and $\mathcal{M}_{23}$ are the mappings defined in Example 3.2. Then the following SO tgd defines the composition of these two mappings:

$$\exists g \left(\forall n \forall c \, (\text{Takes}(n, c) \rightarrow \text{Enrollment}(g(n), c)) \right).$$

□

Up to this point, we have shown that the language of SO tgds is closed under composition, and that the composition of any finite number of mappings specified by st-tgds can be defined by an SO tgd. Thus, SO tgds are a good language when dealing with the composition operator. But, of course, it is natural to ask whether all the features of SO tgds are necessary and whether there exists a smaller language that also has these good properties for composition. Interestingly, it can also be proved that all the features of SO tgds are necessary to deal with the composition operator as every SO tgd defines the composition of a finite number of mappings specified by st-tgds. This fact, which is the converse of Theorem 3.8, shows that SO tgds are exactly the right language for representing the composition of mappings given by st-tgds.

Theorem 3.10   *Every SO tgd defines the composition of a finite number of mappings, each defined by a finite set of st-tgds.*

Example 3.11   Let $\mathbf{R_s}$ be a schema consisting of a unary relation P and $\mathbf{R_t}$ a schema consisting of a binary relation R. Furthermore, assume that the relationship between these schemas is given by the following SO tgd:

$$\sigma \;=\; \exists f \exists g \left(\forall x \, (P(x) \wedge f(x) = g(x) \rightarrow R(f(g(x)), g(f(x)))) \right).$$

We show here the essential steps of an algorithm that, given SO tgd σ, generates a finite sequence of mappings that are given by st-tgds and whose composition is defined by σ.

For the sake of readability, let $\mathbf{R_1}$ be the schema $\mathbf{R_s}$. The algorithm starts by generating a schema $\mathbf{R_2}$, consisting of binary relations F_1, G_1 and of a unary relation P_1, and a mapping $\mathcal{M}_{12} = (\mathbf{R_1}, \mathbf{R_2}, \Sigma_{12})$ that is specified by a set Σ_{12} of st-tgds consisting of the following dependencies:

$$\begin{aligned} P(x) &\rightarrow P_1(x), \\ P(x) &\rightarrow \exists y \, F_1(x, y), \\ P(x) &\rightarrow \exists z \, G_1(x, z). \end{aligned}$$

Intuitively, P_1 is a copy of P, $F_1(x, y)$ indicates that $f(x) = y$, and $G_1(x, y)$ indicates that $g(x) = y$. In particular, the second and third dependencies above have the effect of guaranteeing that $f(x)$ and $g(x)$ are defined for every element x in P, respectively. Then the algorithm generates a schema $\mathbf{R_3}$, consisting of binary relations F_2, G_2 and of a unary relation P_2, and a mapping $\mathcal{M}_{23} = (\mathbf{R_2}, \mathbf{R_3}, \Sigma_{23})$ that is specified by a set Σ_{23} of st-tgds consisting of the following dependencies:

$$
\begin{aligned}
P_1(x) &\rightarrow P_2(x), \\
F_1(x, y) &\rightarrow F_2(x, y), \\
G_1(x, y) &\rightarrow G_2(x, y), \\
F_1(x, y) &\rightarrow \exists u\, G_2(y, u), \\
G_1(x, y) &\rightarrow \exists v\, F_2(y, v).
\end{aligned}
$$

As in the previous case, P_2 is a copy of P_1, $F_2(x, y)$ indicates that $f(x) = y$ and $G_2(x, y)$ indicates that $g(x) = y$. In particular, all the values of f stored in F_1 are also stored in F_2, by the second dependency above, and all the values of g stored in G_1 are also stored in G_2, by the third dependency above. But not only that, the fourth dependency also guarantees that $g(y)$ is defined for all y in the range of f, and the fifth dependency guarantees that $f(y)$ is defined for all y in the range of g. Finally, let $\mathbf{R_4}$ be the schema $\mathbf{R_t}$. Then the algorithm generates a mapping $\mathcal{M}_{34} = (\mathbf{R_3}, \mathbf{R_4}, \Sigma_{34})$ that uses P_2, F_2 and G_2 to populate the target relation R. More precisely, Σ_{34} consists of the following st-tgd:

$$
P(x) \wedge F_2(x, y) \wedge G_2(x, y) \wedge F_2(y, z_1) \wedge G_2(y, z_2) \rightarrow R(z_1, z_2).
$$

The output of the algorithm is the sequence of mapping $\mathcal{M}_{12}, \mathcal{M}_{23}, \mathcal{M}_{34}$, which satisfies that $(\mathcal{M}_{12} \circ \mathcal{M}_{23}) \circ \mathcal{M}_{34}$ is defined by SO tgd σ.

We conclude this example by pointing out that the previous algorithm can be generalized to any SO tgd σ. In fact, if the nesting depth of an SO tgd σ is defined to be the largest depth of the terms that appear in σ, then the generalization of the above algorithm generates a sequence of $r + 1$ mappings when the input is an SO tgd of nesting depth r. $\square$

In this section, we have shown that the language of SO tgds is exactly the right language for representing the composition of mappings given by st-tgds. But up to this point, we have not said anything about the complexity of computing an SO tgd that defines the composition of a sequence of mappings. We conclude this section by saying a few words about this. More specifically, there exists an exponential-time algorithm that given two mappings $\mathcal{M}_{12}$ and $\mathcal{M}_{23}$, each specified by an SO tgd, returns a mapping $\mathcal{M}_{13}$ specified by an SO tgd and equivalent to the composition of $\mathcal{M}_{12}$ and $\mathcal{M}_{23}$. This algorithm, which is a generalization of the procedure presented in Example 3.6, can also be used to compute an SO tgd that defines the composition of two mappings given by st-tgds as every mapping specified by a finite set of st-tgds can be transformed into an equivalent mapping specified by an SO tgd. Moreover, it has been shown that exponentiality is unavoidable in such an algorithm, as there exist mappings $\mathcal{M}_{12}$ and $\mathcal{M}_{23}$, each specified by a finite set of st-tgds, such that every SO tgd that defines the composition of $\mathcal{M}_{12}$ and $\mathcal{M}_{23}$ is of size exponential in the size of $\mathcal{M}_{12}$ and $\mathcal{M}_{23}$.

3.3   INVERTING SCHEMA MAPPING

The inverse operator is another important operator that naturally arises in the development of a framework for managing schema mappings. Once the data has been transferred from the source to the target, the goal of the inverse is to recover the initial source data; if a mapping $\mathcal{M}'$ is an inverse of a mapping $\mathcal{M}$, then $\mathcal{M}'$ should bring the data exchanged through $\mathcal{M}$ back to the source.

In the study of this operator, the key issue is to provide a *good* semantics for this operator, which turned out to be a difficult problem. In this section, we present and compare two of the main proposals for inverting schema mappings that have been considered in the data exchange context, namely the notions of *Fagin-inverse* and *maximum recovery*.

Some of the notions mentioned above are only appropriate for certain classes of mappings. In particular, the following two classes of mappings are used in this section when defining and comparing these notions of inversion. A mapping $\mathcal{M}$ from a schema $\mathbf{R_1}$ to a schema $\mathbf{R_2}$ is said to be *total* if $\text{SOL}_{\mathcal{M}}(S) \neq \emptyset$ for every instance S of $\mathbf{R_1}$ (i.e., all instances have solutions). A mapping $\mathcal{M}$ is said to be *closed-down on the left* if $(S_1, S_2) \in \mathcal{M}$ and $S_1' \subseteq S_1$ imply that $(S_1', S_2) \in \mathcal{M}$. Furthermore, whenever a mapping is specified by a set of formulas, we consider source instances as just containing constants values, and target instances as containing constants and null values. This is a natural assumption in a data exchange context since target instances generated as a result of exchanging data may be *incomplete*, thus, null values are used as place-holders for unknown information.

3.3.1   A FIRST DEFINITION OF INVERSE

We start by considering the first notion of inverse for schema mappings proposed in the literature, that we call Fagin-inverse in this chapter. Roughly speaking, the definition of this notion is based on the idea that a mapping composed with its inverse should be equal to the identity schema mapping. Thus, given a schema $\mathbf{R}$, an identity schema mapping $\overline{\text{Id}}_{\mathbf{R}}$ is first define as $\{(S_1, S_2) \mid S_1, S_2$ are instances of $\mathbf{R}$ and $S_1 \subseteq S_2\}$, and then the notion of Fagin-inverse is defined as follows.

Definition 3.12   (Fagin-inverse).   Let $\mathcal{M}$ be a mapping from a schema $\mathbf{R_1}$ to a schema $\mathbf{R_2}$, and $\mathcal{M}'$ a mapping from $\mathbf{R_2}$ to $\mathbf{R_1}$. Then $\mathcal{M}'$ is a *Fagin-inverse* of $\mathcal{M}$ if $\mathcal{M} \circ \mathcal{M}' = \overline{\text{Id}}_{\mathbf{R_1}}$.   □

It is important to notice that $\overline{\text{Id}}_{\mathbf{R}}$ is not the usual identity relation over $\mathbf{R}$. In fact, this identity is appropriate for mappings that are total and closed-down on the left and, in particular, for the class of mappings specified by st-tgds.

Example 3.13   Let $\mathbf{R_1}$ be a schema consisting of a unary relation S, $\mathbf{R_2}$ a schema consisting of unary relations U and V, and $\mathcal{M}$ a mapping from $\mathbf{R_1}$ to $\mathbf{R_2}$ specified by st-tgds $S(x) \rightarrow U(x)$ and $S(x) \rightarrow V(x)$. Intuitively, $\mathcal{M}$ is Fagin-invertible since all the information in the source relation S is transferred to both relations U and V in the target. In fact, the mapping $\mathcal{M}'$ specified by dependency $U(x) \rightarrow S(x)$ is a Fagin-inverse of $\mathcal{M}$ since $\mathcal{M} \circ \mathcal{M}' = \overline{\text{Id}}_{\mathbf{R_1}}$. But not only that, the mapping $\mathcal{M}''$ specified by dependency $V(x) \rightarrow S(x)$ is also a Fagin-inverse of $\mathcal{M}$, which shows that there need not be a unique Fagin-inverse.   □

A first fundamental question about any schema mapping operator is for which class of mappings it is defined. In particular, for the case of the inverse operator, one would like to know for which classes of mappings it is guaranteed to exist. To answer this question, necessary and sufficient conditions for the existence of the distinct inverse notions have been developed. Here, we present one such condition for the case of the notion of Fagin-inverse, and we use it to show that Fagin-inverses are not guaranteed to exist for the class of mappings specified by st-tgds. More precisely, a mapping $\mathcal{M}$ from a schema $\mathbf{R_1}$ to a schema $\mathbf{R_2}$ is said to satisfy the *unique-solutions property* if for every pair of instances S_1, S_2 of $\mathbf{R_1}$, if $\textsc{Sol}_{\mathcal{M}}(S_1) = \textsc{Sol}_{\mathcal{M}}(S_2)$, then $S_1 = S_2$. The following proposition shows that the unique-solutions property is a necessary condition for the existence of Fagin-inverses.

Proposition 3.14   *Let $\mathcal{M}$ be a total and closed-down on the left mapping. If $\mathcal{M}$ is Fagin-invertible, then $\mathcal{M}$ satisfies the unique-solutions property.*

Proof. Assume that $\mathcal{M}$ is a mapping from a schema $\mathbf{R_1}$ to a schema $\mathbf{R_2}$, and let $\mathcal{M}'$ be a mapping from $\mathbf{R_2}$ to $\mathbf{R_1}$ such that $\mathcal{M} \circ \mathcal{M}' = \overline{\textsf{Id}}_{\mathbf{R_1}}$ (such a mapping exists since $\mathcal{M}$ is Fagin-invertible). Moreover, assume that S_1 and S_2 are instances of $\mathbf{R_1}$ such that $\textsc{Sol}_{\mathcal{M}}(S_1) = \textsc{Sol}_{\mathcal{M}}(S_2)$. We need to show that $S_1 = S_2$.

Given that $\textsc{Sol}_{\mathcal{M}}(S_1) = \textsc{Sol}_{\mathcal{M}}(S_2)$, we have that $\textsc{Sol}_{\mathcal{M} \circ \mathcal{M}'}(S_1) = \textsc{Sol}_{\mathcal{M} \circ \mathcal{M}'}(S_2)$. Thus, given that $\mathcal{M} \circ \mathcal{M}' = \overline{\textsf{Id}}_{\mathbf{R_1}}$, we conclude that $\textsc{Sol}_{\overline{\textsf{Id}}_{\mathbf{R_1}}}(S_1) = \textsc{Sol}_{\overline{\textsf{Id}}_{\mathbf{R_1}}}(S_2)$. Therefore, from the fact that $S_1 \in \textsc{Sol}_{\overline{\textsf{Id}}_{\mathbf{R_1}}}(S_1)$ and $S_2 \in \textsc{Sol}_{\overline{\textsf{Id}}_{\mathbf{R_1}}}(S_2)$, we conclude that $S_1 \in \textsc{Sol}_{\overline{\textsf{Id}}_{\mathbf{R_1}}}(S_2)$ and $S_2 \in \textsc{Sol}_{\overline{\textsf{Id}}_{\mathbf{R_1}}}(S_1)$. But this implies that $(S_2, S_1) \in \overline{\textsf{Id}}_{\mathbf{R_1}}$ and $(S_1, S_2) \in \overline{\textsf{Id}}_{\mathbf{R_1}}$, and, hence, we conclude from the definition of $\overline{\textsf{Id}}_{\mathbf{R_1}}$ that $S_2 \subseteq S_1$ and $S_1 \subseteq S_2$. This concludes the proof of the proposition. □

Proposition 3.14 tell us that the spaces of solutions for distinct source instances under a Fagin-invertible mapping must be distinct. Thus, one can prove that a mapping does not admit a Fagin-inverse by showing that it does not satisfy the preceding condition.

Example 3.15   Let $\mathbf{R_1}$ be a schema consisting of a binary relation R, $\mathbf{R_2}$ a schema consisting of a unary relation T, and $\mathcal{M}$ a mapping from $\mathbf{R_1}$ to $\mathbf{R_2}$ specified by st-tgd $R(x, y) \rightarrow T(x)$. Intuitively, $\mathcal{M}$ has no Fagin-inverse since $\mathcal{M}$ only transfers from source to target the information about the first component of R. In fact, it can be formally proved that this mapping is not Fagin-invertible as follows. Let S_1 and S_2 be instances of $\mathbf{R_1}$ such that:

$$R^{S_1} = \{(1, 2)\} \quad \text{and} \quad R^{S_2} = \{(1, 3)\}.$$

Then we have that $\textsc{Sol}_{\mathcal{M}}(S_1) = \textsc{Sol}_{\mathcal{M}}(S_2)$, which implies that $\mathcal{M}$ does not satisfies the unique-solutions property since $S_1 \neq S_2$. □

From the preceding example, we obtain that:

Corollary 3.16   *There exists a mapping $\mathcal{M}$ specified by a finite set of st-tgds that does not admit a Fagin-inverse.*

Although the unique-solutions property is a useful tool for establishing non Fagin-invertibility, it can be shown that it does not characterize this notion. In fact, the following example shows that the unique-solutions property is not a sufficient condition for Fagin-invertibility even for the class of mappings specified by st-tgds.

Example 3.17   Let $\mathbf{R_1}$ be a schema consisting of unary relations A and B, $\mathbf{R_2}$ a schema consisting of a binary relation R and a unary relation C, and $\mathcal{M}$ a mapping from $\mathbf{R_1}$ to $\mathbf{R_2}$ specified by st-tgds:

$$
\begin{aligned}
A(x) &\rightarrow R(x, x), \\
B(x) &\rightarrow \exists y\, R(x, y), \\
A(x) \wedge B(x) &\rightarrow C(x).
\end{aligned}
$$

Next, we show that $\mathcal{M}$ satisfies the unique-solutions property, but it is not Fagin-invertible. Assume that S_1 and S_2 are distinct instances of $\mathbf{R_1}$. Next, we show that $\text{SOL}_{\mathcal{M}}(S_1) \neq \text{SOL}_{\mathcal{M}}(S_2)$ by considering the following cases.

(1) Assume that there exists $a \in A^{S_1}$ such that $a \notin A^{S_2}$, and let T_2 be the canonical universal solution for S_2 under $\mathcal{M}$. Then we have that $(a, a) \notin R^{T_2}$, and, therefore, T_2 is not a solution for S_1 under $\mathcal{M}$. We conclude that $\text{SOL}_{\mathcal{M}}(S_1) \neq \text{SOL}_{\mathcal{M}}(S_2)$.

(2) Assume that there exists $a \in A^{S_2}$ such that $a \notin A^{S_1}$. Then it can be shown that $\text{SOL}_{\mathcal{M}}(S_1) \neq \text{SOL}_{\mathcal{M}}(S_2)$ as in the previous case.

(3) Assume that $A^{S_1} = A^{S_2}$, and that there exists $b \in B^{S_1}$ such that $b \notin A^{S_1}$ and $b \notin B^{S_2}$. Then let T_2 be the canonical universal solution for S_2 under $\mathcal{M}$. Given that $b \notin A^{S_2}$, we have that R^{T_2} does not contain any tuple of the form $R(b, c)$, and, therefore, T_2 is not a solution for S_1 under $\mathcal{M}$. We conclude that $\text{SOL}_{\mathcal{M}}(S_1) \neq \text{SOL}_{\mathcal{M}}(S_2)$.

(4) Assume that $A^{S_1} = A^{S_2}$, and that there exists $b \in B^{S_2}$ such that $b \notin A^{S_1}$ and $b \notin B^{S_1}$. Then we conclude that $\text{SOL}_{\mathcal{M}}(S_1) \neq \text{SOL}_{\mathcal{M}}(S_2)$ as in the previous case.

(5) Assume that $A^{S_1} = A^{S_2}$, and that there exists $b \in B^{S_1}$ such that $b \in A^{S_1}$ and $b \notin B^{S_2}$. Then let T_2 be the canonical universal solution for S_2 under $\mathcal{M}$. Given that $b \notin B^{S_2}$, we have that $b \notin C^{T_2}$, and, therefore, T_2 is not a solution for S_1 under $\mathcal{M}$. We conclude that $\text{SOL}_{\mathcal{M}}(S_1) \neq \text{SOL}_{\mathcal{M}}(S_2)$.

(6) Finally, assume that $A^{S_1} = A^{S_2}$, and that there exists $b \in B^{S_2}$ such that $b \in A^{S_1}$ and $b \notin B^{S_1}$. Then we conclude that $\text{SOL}_{\mathcal{M}}(S_1) \neq \text{SOL}_{\mathcal{M}}(S_2)$ as in the previous case.

Now, for the sake of contradiction, assume that $\mathcal{M}$ is a Fagin-invertible mapping, and let $\mathcal{M}'$ be a mapping from $\mathbf{R_2}$ to $\mathbf{R_1}$ such that $\mathcal{M} \circ \mathcal{M}' = \overline{\mathrm{Id}}_{\mathbf{R_1}}$. Then for every pair S_1, S_2 of instances of $\mathbf{R_1}$ such that $\mathrm{Sol}_{\mathcal{M}}(S_1) \subseteq \mathrm{Sol}_{\mathcal{M}}(S_2)$, it holds that $S_2 \subseteq S_1$. To see why this is the case, first notice that if $\mathrm{Sol}_{\mathcal{M}}(S_1) \subseteq \mathrm{Sol}_{\mathcal{M}}(S_2)$, then $\mathrm{Sol}_{\mathcal{M} \circ \mathcal{M}'}(S_1) \subseteq \mathrm{Sol}_{\mathcal{M} \circ \mathcal{M}'}(S_2)$. Thus, given that $\mathcal{M} \circ \mathcal{M}' = \overline{\mathrm{Id}}_{\mathbf{R_1}}$, we have that $\mathrm{Sol}_{\overline{\mathrm{Id}}_{\mathbf{R_1}}}(S_1) \subseteq \mathrm{Sol}_{\overline{\mathrm{Id}}_{\mathbf{R_1}}}(S_2)$. Hence, from the fact that $S_1 \in \mathrm{Sol}_{\overline{\mathrm{Id}}_{\mathbf{R_1}}}(S_1)$, we conclude that $S_1 \in \mathrm{Sol}_{\overline{\mathrm{Id}}_{\mathbf{R_1}}}(S_2)$, and, therefore, $S_2 \subseteq S_1$.

Next, we use the property shown above to obtain a contradiction. Assume that S_1 and S_2 are instances of $\mathbf{R_1}$ such that:

$$A^{S_1} = \{1\} \qquad A^{S_2} = \emptyset$$
$$B^{S_1} = \emptyset \qquad B^{S_2} = \{1\}$$

Then we have that $\mathrm{Sol}_{\mathcal{M}}(S_1) \subseteq \mathrm{Sol}_{\mathcal{M}}(S_2)$, which contradicts the property shown above since $S_2 \not\subseteq S_1$. $\square$

In Example 3.17, we introduced a second condition that Fagin-invertible mappings satisfy and that is stronger than the unique-solutions property. Formally, a mapping $\mathcal{M}$ from a schema $\mathbf{R_1}$ to a schema $\mathbf{R_2}$ is said to satisfy the *subset property* if for every pair S_1, S_2 of instances of $\mathbf{R_1}$, if $\mathrm{Sol}_{\mathcal{M}}(S_1) \subseteq \mathrm{Sol}_{\mathcal{M}}(S_2)$, then $S_2 \subseteq S_1$. It turns out that this condition is a necessary and sufficient condition for the existence of Fagin-inverses for the class of mappings specified by st-tgds.

Theorem 3.18   *Let $\mathcal{M}$ be a mapping specified by a finite set of st-tgds. Then $\mathcal{M}$ is Fagin-invertible if and only if $\mathcal{M}$ satisfies the subset property.*

The previous result does not extend to the entire class of total and closed-down on the left mappings. In fact, a characterization of Fagin invertibility requires of a stronger condition, which is defined as follows. Let $\mathcal{M}$ be a mapping from a schema $\mathbf{R_1}$ to a schema $\mathbf{R_2}$, S be an instance of $\mathbf{R_1}$ and T be an instance of $\mathbf{R_2}$. Then T is a *strong witness* for S under $\mathcal{M}$ if for every instance S' of $\mathbf{R_1}$ such that $T \in \mathrm{Sol}_{\mathcal{M}}(S')$, it holds that $S' \subseteq S$. If T is also a solution, we call it a *strong witness solution*. Strong witness solutions exist for Fagin-invertible mappings that are specified by st-tgds.

Proposition 3.19   *Let $\mathcal{M}$ be a Fagin-invertible mapping from a schema $\mathbf{R_1}$ to a schema $\mathbf{R_2}$ that is specified by a set of st-tgds. Then for every instance S of $\mathbf{R_1}$, each universal solution T for S under $\mathcal{M}$ is also a strong witness solution for S under $\mathcal{M}$.*

Proof. Let S be an instance of $\mathbf{R_1}$ and T a universal solution for S under $\mathcal{M}$ (such a solution exists since $\mathcal{M}$ is specified by a set of st-tgds). Assume that S' is an instance of $\mathbf{R_1}$ such that $T \in \mathrm{Sol}_{\mathcal{M}}(S')$. Next, we show that $S' \subseteq S$.

Given that $T \in \mathrm{Sol}_{\mathcal{M}}(S')$, we have that $\mathrm{Sol}_{\mathcal{M}}(S) \subseteq \mathrm{Sol}_{\mathcal{M}}(S')$. To see why this is the case, let T' be a solution for S under $\mathcal{M}$. Given that T is a universal solution for S under $\mathcal{M}$, we have that there exists a homomorphism from T into T'. Thus, given that $T \in \text{SOL}_{\mathcal{M}}(S')$ and $\mathcal{M}$ is closed under target homomorphisms[2], we conclude that $T' \in \text{SOL}_{\mathcal{M}}(S')$.

Since $\mathcal{M}$ is Fagin-invertible, we know that $\mathcal{M}$ satisfies the subset-property. Thus, given that $\text{SOL}_{\mathcal{M}}(S) \subseteq \text{SOL}_{\mathcal{M}}(S')$, we have that $S' \subseteq S$, which concludes the proof of the proposition.   □

In the following theorem, it is shown that the notion of strong witness can be used to characterize Fagin-invertibility for the class of mappings that are total and closed-down on the left.

Theorem 3.20   *Let $\mathcal{M}$ be a total and closed-down on the left mapping from a schema $\mathbf{R_1}$ to a schema $\mathbf{R_2}$. Then $\mathcal{M}$ is Fagin-invertible if and only if every instance of $\mathbf{R_1}$ has a strong witness solution under $\mathcal{M}$.*

Given that Fagin-inverses are not guaranteed to exist for the class of mappings specified by st-tgds, a second fundamental question about this notion of inverse is whether Fagin-invertibility is a decidable condition for this class of mappings. Interestingly, the subset property can be used to prove that this is indeed a decidable condition: if a mapping $\mathcal{M}$ specified by a set of st-tgds does not have a Fagin-inverse, then there exists a polynomial-size counterexample showing that $\mathcal{M}$ does not satisfy the subset property.

Theorem 3.21   *The problem of checking, given a mapping $\mathcal{M}$ specified by a set of st-tgds, whether $\mathcal{M}$ is Fagin-invertible is* coNP-*complete.*

Proof. We show here the membership of the problem in coNP, and leave coNP-hardness as an exercise for the reader. Given a mapping $\mathcal{M} = (\mathbf{R_1}, \mathbf{R_2}, \Sigma_{12})$ that is not Fagin-invertible, a pair (S_1, S_2) of instances of $\mathbf{R_1}$ is said to be a witness for the non Fagin-invertibility of $\mathcal{M}$ if $\text{SOL}_{\mathcal{M}}(S_1) \subseteq \text{SOL}_{\mathcal{M}}(S_2)$ but $S_2 \not\subseteq S_1$ (notice that such a pair shows that $\mathcal{M}$ does not satisfy the subset property). Then it is shown here that for every mapping $\mathcal{M}$ specified by a set of st-tgds, if $\mathcal{M}$ is not Fagin-invertible, then there exists a witness (S_1, S_2) for the non Fagin-invertibility of $\mathcal{M}$ such that $\|S_1\| + \|S_2\|$ is $O(\|\Sigma_{12}\|^2)$, from which the membership of the problem in coNP immediately follows.

Let $\mathcal{M} = (\mathbf{R_1}, \mathbf{R_2}, \Sigma_{12})$, where Σ_{12} is a set of st-tgds, and assume that $\mathcal{M}$ is not Fagin-invertible. Then we have by Theorem 3.18 that there exist instances S_1, S_2 of $\mathbf{R_1}$ such that $\text{SOL}_{\mathcal{M}}(S_1) \subseteq \text{SOL}_{\mathcal{M}}(S_2)$ but $S_2 \not\subseteq S_1$. Thus, there exist P in $\mathbf{R_1}$ and $t_0 \in P^{S_2}$ such that $t_0 \notin P^{S_1}$. Let $S_2^\star$ be an instance of $\mathbf{R_1}$ consisting only of fact $P(t_0)$, that is, $P^{S_2^\star} = \{t_0\}$ and $R^{S_2^\star} = \emptyset$ for all the other relations R in $\mathbf{R_1}$. Since Σ_{12} is a set of st-tgds, we have that:

$$\text{SOL}_{\mathcal{M}}(S_2) \quad \subseteq \quad \text{SOL}_{\mathcal{M}}(S_2^\star).$$

Hence, $\text{SOL}_{\mathcal{M}}(S_1) \subseteq \text{SOL}_{\mathcal{M}}(S_2^\star)$ and $S_2^\star \not\subseteq S_1$, which shows that $(S_1, S_2^\star)$ is also a witness for the non Fagin-invertibility of mapping $\mathcal{M}$. Now let T_1, $T_2^\star$ be the canonical universal solutions for S_1 and

---

[2]A mapping $\mathcal{M}$ is closed under target homomorphisms if for every $(S, T) \in \mathcal{M}$ and T' such that there exists a homomorphism from T to T', it holds that $(S, T') \in \mathcal{M}$.

$S_2^\star$ under $\mathcal{M}$, respectively. Given that $T_1 \in \text{Sol}_\mathcal{M}(S_1)$, we have that $T_1 \in \text{Sol}_\mathcal{M}(S_2^\star)$, and, therefore, there exists a homomorphism h from $T_2^\star$ to T_1. We use h to construct the desired quadratic-size witness for the non Fagin-invertibility of mapping $\mathcal{M}$. More precisely, let $S_1^\star$ be an instance of $\mathbf{R_1}$ defined as follows. For every R in $\mathbf{R_2}$ and tuple $t \in R^{T_2^\star}$, choose a st-tgd $\varphi(\bar{x}) \to \exists \bar{y}\, \psi(\bar{x}, \bar{y})$ and tuples $\bar{a}, \bar{b}$ such that (1) $\varphi(\bar{x}) \to \exists \bar{y}\, \psi(\bar{x}, \bar{y})$ is a st-tgd in Σ_{12}, $\bar{a}$ is a tuple of values from $\text{Dom}(S_1)$ and $\bar{b}$ is a tuple of values from $\text{Dom}(T_1)$, (2) $\varphi(\bar{a})$ holds in S_1, (3) $\psi(\bar{a}, \bar{b})$ holds in T_1, and (4) $R(h(t))$ is a conjunct in $\psi(\bar{a}, \bar{b})$. It should be noticed that such a tuple exists since (S_1, T_1) satisfies Σ_{12} and $R(h(t))$ is a fact in T_1 (given that h is a homomorphism from $T_2^\star$ to T_1). Then include all the conjuncts of $\varphi(\bar{a})$ as facts of $S_1^\star$. Next, we show that $(S_1^\star, S_2^\star)$ is a witness for the non Fagin-invertibility of $\mathcal{M}$ and $\|S_1^\star\| + \|S_2^\star\|$ is $O(\|\Sigma_{12}\|^2)$.

Let $T_1^\star$ be the canonical universal solution for $S_1^\star$ under $\mathcal{M}$. By definition of $S_1^\star$, we have that the homomorphism h mentioned above is also a homomorphism from $T_2^\star$ to $T_1^\star$. Thus, given that $T_1^\star$ is a universal solution for $S_1^\star$ under $\mathcal{M}$ and $\mathcal{M}$ is closed under target homomorphisms, we conclude that $\text{Sol}_\mathcal{M}(S_1^\star) \subseteq \text{Sol}_\mathcal{M}(S_2^\star)$. Moreover, given that $S_1^\star \subseteq S_1$, we also have that $S_2^\star \not\subseteq S_1^\star$ and, hence, $(S_1^\star, S_2^\star)$ is a witness for the non Fagin-invertibility of $\mathcal{M}$. Finally, given that $S_2^\star$ consists of only one fact, we have that $\|T_2^\star\|$ is bounded by $\|\Sigma_{12}\|$. Therefore, given that the number of tuples that are included in $S_1^\star$ for each fact $R(t)$ in $T_2^\star$ is bounded by $\|\Sigma_{12}\|$, we have that $\|S_1^\star\|$ is bounded by $\|\Sigma_{12}\|^2$. Thus, it holds that $\|S_1^\star\| + \|S_2^\star\|$ is $O(\|\Sigma_{12}\|^2)$, which concludes the proof of the theorem. $\square$

A problem related to checking Fagin-invertibility is to check, for mappings $\mathcal{M}$ and $\mathcal{M}'$, whether $\mathcal{M}'$ is a Fagin-inverse of $\mathcal{M}$. Somewhat surprisingly, this problem is undecidable even for the class of mappings specified by st-tgds.

Theorem 3.22 *The problem of verifying, given mappings $\mathcal{M} = (\mathbf{R_1}, \mathbf{R_2}, \Sigma_{12})$ and $\mathcal{M}' = (\mathbf{R_2}, \mathbf{R_1}, \Sigma_{21})$ with Σ_{12} and Σ_{21} finite sets of st-tgds, whether $\mathcal{M}'$ is a Fagin-inverse of $\mathcal{M}$ is undecidable.*

A fundamental, and arguably the most important, issue about any notion of inverse is the problem of computing an inverse for a given mapping. In the next section, we introduce the notion of maximum recovery, which has also been proposed as a notion of inverse for schema mappings, and then we study the issue of computing inverses in Section 3.3.3. In particular, we present a unified algorithm based on query rewriting that computes not only Fagin-inverses but also maximum recoveries.

3.3.2 BRINGING EXCHANGED DATA BACK: THE RECOVERY OF A SCHEMA MAPPING

As we mentioned before, a drawback of the notion of Fagin-inverse is that not every mapping specified by a set of st-tgds is guaranteed to have an inverse under this notion. In this section, we present the concepts of recovery and maximum recovery that were introduced to overcome this limitation.

The notion of recovery is defined by following a different approach to that of Fagin-inverse. In fact, the main goal behind this notion is not to define an inverse operator but, instead, to give a formal definition for what it means for a mapping $\mathcal{M}'$ to recover *sound information* with respect to a mapping $\mathcal{M}$. Such a mapping $\mathcal{M}'$ is called a recovery of $\mathcal{M}$. But given that, in general, there may exist many possible recoveries for a given mapping, it is also necessary to introduce a way to compare alternative recoveries. This naturally gives rise to the notion of maximum recovery, which is a mapping that brings back the maximum amount of sound information.

Let $\mathcal{M}$ be a mapping from a schema $\mathbf{R}_1$ to a schema $\mathbf{R}_2$, and $\mathrm{Id}_{\mathbf{R}_1}$ the identity schema mapping over $\mathbf{R}_1$, that is, $\mathrm{Id}_{\mathbf{R}_1} = \{(S, S) \mid S \in \mathrm{Inst}(\mathbf{R}_1)\}$. When trying to invert $\mathcal{M}$, the ideal would be to find a mapping $\mathcal{M}'$ from $\mathbf{R}_2$ to $\mathbf{R}_1$ such that $\mathcal{M} \circ \mathcal{M}' = \mathrm{Id}_{\mathbf{R}_1}$; if such a mapping exists, then we know that if we use $\mathcal{M}$ to exchange data, the application of $\mathcal{M}'$ gives as result exactly the initial source instance. Unfortunately, in most cases this ideal is impossible to reach (for example, for the case of mappings specified by st-tgds). But then at least one would like to find a schema mapping $\mathcal{M}_2$ that does not forbid the possibility of recovering the initial source data. This gives rise to the notion of recovery. In what follows, we refer to the *domain* of a mapping $\mathcal{M}$, denoted by $\mathrm{Dom}(\mathcal{M})$, as the set of source instances S that have solutions under $\mathcal{M}$ ($\mathrm{Sol}_{\mathcal{M}}(S) \neq \emptyset$).

Definition 3.23   (Recovery).   Let $\mathcal{M}$ be a mapping from a schema $\mathbf{R}_1$ to a schema $\mathbf{R}_2$, and $\mathcal{M}'$ a mapping from $\mathbf{R}_2$ to $\mathbf{R}_1$. Then $\mathcal{M}'$ is a *recovery* of $\mathcal{M}$ if for every instance $S \in \mathrm{Dom}(\mathcal{M})$, it holds that $(S, S) \in \mathcal{M} \circ \mathcal{M}'$.   □

Being a recovery is a sound but mild requirement. Indeed, a schema mapping $\mathcal{M}$ from a schema $\mathbf{R}_1$ to a schema $\mathbf{R}_2$ always has as recoveries, for example, mappings $\mathcal{M}_1 = \mathrm{Inst}(\mathbf{R}_2) \times \mathrm{Inst}(\mathbf{R}_1)$ and $\mathcal{M}_2 = \mathcal{M}^{-1} = \{(T, S) \mid (S, T) \in \mathcal{M}\}$. If one has to choose between $\mathcal{M}_1$ and $\mathcal{M}_2$ as a recovery of $\mathcal{M}$, then one would probably choose $\mathcal{M}_2$ since the space of possible solutions for an instance S under $\mathcal{M} \circ \mathcal{M}_2$ is smaller than under $\mathcal{M} \circ \mathcal{M}_1$. In general, if $\mathcal{M}'$ is a recovery of $\mathcal{M}$, then the smaller the space of solutions generated by $\mathcal{M} \circ \mathcal{M}'$, the more informative $\mathcal{M}'$ is about the initial source instances. This naturally gives rise to the notion of maximum recovery.

Definition 3.24   (Maximum recovery).   Let $\mathcal{M}$ be a mapping from a schema $\mathbf{R}_1$ to a schema $\mathbf{R}_2$, and $\mathcal{M}'$ a mapping from $\mathbf{R}_2$ to $\mathbf{R}_1$. Then $\mathcal{M}'$ is a *maximum recovery* of $\mathcal{M}$ if:

(1) $\mathcal{M}'$ is a recovery of $\mathcal{M}$, and

(2) for every recovery $\mathcal{M}''$ of $\mathcal{M}$, it holds that $\mathcal{M} \circ \mathcal{M}' \subseteq \mathcal{M} \circ \mathcal{M}''$.

□

Example 3.25   Let $\mathbf{R}_1$ be a schema consisting of a binary relation E, $\mathbf{R}_2$ a schema consisting of a binary relation F and a unary relation G, and $\mathcal{M} = (\mathbf{R}_1, \mathbf{R}_2, \Sigma)$ with Σ a set of st-tgds consisting of the following dependency:

$$E(x, z) \wedge E(z, y) \quad \rightarrow \quad F(x, y) \wedge G(z). \tag{3.9}$$

Let $\mathcal{M}_1$ be a mapping from $\mathbf{R}_2$ to $\mathbf{R}_1$ specified by tgd:

$$F(x, y) \quad \rightarrow \quad \exists z \, (E(x, z) \wedge E(z, y)). \tag{3.10}$$

It is straightforward to prove that $\mathcal{M}_1$ is a recovery of $\mathcal{M}$. In fact, if S is an instance of $\mathbf{R}_1$ and T is the canonical universal solution for S under $\mathcal{M}$, then we have that $(S, T) \in \mathcal{M}$ and $(T, S) \in \mathcal{M}_1$, from which we conclude that $(S, S) \in \mathcal{M} \circ \mathcal{M}_1$. Similarly, if $\mathcal{M}_2$ is a mapping from $\mathbf{R}_2$ to $\mathbf{R}_1$ specified by tgd:

$$G(z) \quad \rightarrow \quad \exists x \exists y \, (E(x, z) \wedge E(z, y)), \tag{3.11}$$

then we also have that $\mathcal{M}_2$ is a recovery of $\mathcal{M}$. On the other hand, if $\mathcal{M}_3$ is a mapping from $\mathbf{R}_2$ to $\mathbf{R}_1$ specified by tgd:

$$F(x, y) \wedge G(z) \quad \rightarrow \quad E(x, z) \wedge E(z, y), \tag{3.12}$$

then we have that $\mathcal{M}_3$ is not a recovery of $\mathcal{M}$. To see why this is the case, consider an instance S of $\mathbf{R}_1$ such that:

$$E^S \quad = \quad \{(1, 1), (2, 2)\}.$$

Next, we show that $(S, S) \notin \mathcal{M} \circ \mathcal{M}_3$. By the sake of contradiction, assume that $(S, S) \in \mathcal{M} \circ \mathcal{M}_3$, and let T be an instance of $\mathbf{R}_2$ such that $(S, T) \in \mathcal{M}$ and $(T, S) \in \mathcal{M}_3$. Given that (S, T) satisfies st-tgd (3.9), we have that $(1, 1)$, $(2, 2)$ are elements of F^T and $1, 2$ are elements of G^T. But then given that (T, S) satisfies tgd (3.12), we conclude that the tuples $(1, 2)$, $(2, 1)$ are elements of E^S, which leads to a contradiction.

Finally, let $\mathcal{M}_4$ be a mapping from $\mathbf{R}_2$ to $\mathbf{R}_1$ specified by tgds (3.10) and (3.11). In this case, it is possible to prove that $\mathcal{M}_4$ is a maximum recovery of $\mathcal{M}$. In fact, next, we introduce some characterizations of the notion of maximum recovery that can be used to prove this fact.   □

To check whether a mapping $\mathcal{M}'$ is a Fagin-inverse of a mapping $\mathcal{M}$, a condition that depends only on $\mathcal{M}$ and $\mathcal{M}'$ needs to be checked, namely that the composition of $\mathcal{M}$ with $\mathcal{M}'$ is equal to the identity mapping. On the other hand, verifying whether a mapping $\mathcal{M}'$ is a maximum recovery of a mapping $\mathcal{M}$ requires comparing $\mathcal{M}'$ with every other recovery of $\mathcal{M}$. Given that such a test is more complicated, it would be desirable to have an alternative condition for this notion that depends only on the input mappings. The next proposition gives one such condition.

Proposition 3.26   *Let $\mathcal{M}$ be a mapping from a schema $\mathbf{R}_1$ to a schema $\mathbf{R}_2$, and $\mathcal{M}'$ be a recovery of $\mathcal{M}$. Then $\mathcal{M}'$ is a maximum recovery of $\mathcal{M}$ if and only if:*

(1) for every $(S_1, S_2) \in \mathcal{M} \circ \mathcal{M}'$, it holds that $S_2 \in \mathrm{Dom}(\mathcal{M})$, and

(2) $\mathcal{M} = \mathcal{M} \circ \mathcal{M}' \circ \mathcal{M}$.

Next, we use Proposition 3.26 to prove that the claims in Example 3.25 are indeed correct. But before doing this, we give some intuition about the conditions in Proposition 3.26. The first such condition tells us that if an instance S is not in the domain of a mapping $\mathcal{M}$, then a maximum recovery of $\mathcal{M}$ should not recover information about this instance. The second condition in Proposition 3.26 is a desirable property for an inverse mapping. Intuitively, given a mapping $\mathcal{M}$ from a schema $\mathbf{R_1}$ to a schema $\mathbf{R_2}$ and a mapping $\mathcal{M}'$ from $\mathbf{R_2}$ to $\mathbf{R_1}$, mapping $\mathcal{M}'$ does not lose information when bringing back the data exchanged by $\mathcal{M}$, if the space of solutions of every instance of $\mathbf{R_1}$ does not change after computing $\mathcal{M} \circ \mathcal{M}'$. That is, for every instance S of $\mathbf{R_1}$, it should hold that $\text{SOL}_{\mathcal{M}}(S) = \text{SOL}_{\mathcal{M} \circ \mathcal{M}' \circ \mathcal{M}}(S)$ (or more succinctly, $\mathcal{M} = \mathcal{M} \circ \mathcal{M}' \circ \mathcal{M}$). In general, recoveries do not satisfy this condition, but Proposition 3.26 shows that maximum recoveries satisfy it. And not only that, it also shows that the notion of maximum recovery can be characterized in terms of this condition.

Example 3.27 (Example 3.25 continued)   Recall that mapping $\mathcal{M}$ in Example 3.25 is specified by the following st-tgd:

$$E(x, z) \wedge E(z, y) \quad \rightarrow \quad F(x, y) \wedge G(z),$$

while recovery $\mathcal{M}_4$ of $\mathcal{M}$ is specified by the following tgds:

$$\begin{aligned} F(x, y) \quad &\rightarrow \quad \exists z\, (E(x, z) \wedge E(z, y)), \\ G(z) \quad &\rightarrow \quad \exists x \exists y\, (E(x, z) \wedge E(z, y)). \end{aligned}$$

Next, we use Proposition 3.26 to show that $\mathcal{M}_4$ is a maximum recovery of $\mathcal{M}$. Given that $\mathcal{M}_4$ is a recovery of $\mathcal{M}$, we have that $\mathcal{M} \subseteq \mathcal{M} \circ \mathcal{M}_4 \circ \mathcal{M}$. Thus, given that $\text{DOM}(\mathcal{M}) = \mathbf{R_1}$, we conclude from Proposition 3.26 that to prove that $\mathcal{M}_4$ is a maximum recovery of $\mathcal{M}$, we only need to show that $\mathcal{M} \circ \mathcal{M}_4 \circ \mathcal{M} \subseteq \mathcal{M}$.

Let $(S, T) \in \mathcal{M} \circ \mathcal{M}_4 \circ \mathcal{M}$. To prove that $(S, T) \in \mathcal{M}$, we need to show that (S, T) satisfies the st-tgd that specifies $\mathcal{M}$, that is, we have to prove that for every pair of tuples (a, b), (b, c) in E^S, where a, b, c are not necessarily distinct elements, it holds that $(a, c) \in F^T$ and $b \in G^T$. To prove this, first notice that given that $(S, T) \in \mathcal{M} \circ \mathcal{M}_4 \circ \mathcal{M}$, there exist instances S_1 of $\mathbf{R_1}$ and T_1 of $\mathbf{R_2}$ such that $(S, T_1) \in \mathcal{M}$, $(T_1, S_1) \in \mathcal{M}_4$ and $(S_1, T) \in \mathcal{M}$. Thus, given that (a, b), (b, c) are elements of E^S, we conclude that $(a, c) \in F^{T_1}$ and $b \in G^{T_1}$. Hence, from the definition of $\mathcal{M}_4$ and the fact that $(T_1, S_1) \in \mathcal{M}_4$, we conclude that there exist elements d, e and f such that:

$$\{(a, d), (d, c), (e, b), (b, f)\} \quad \subseteq \quad E^{S_1}.$$

Therefore, given that $(S_1, T) \in \mathcal{M}$, we conclude that $(a, c) \in F^T$ and $b \in G^T$, which was to be shown.

On the other hand, it is claimed in Example 3.25 that the mapping $\mathcal{M}_1$ specified by dependency $F(x, y) \rightarrow \exists z\, (E(x, z) \wedge E(z, y))$ is not a maximum recovery of $\mathcal{M}$ (although it is a recovery of $\mathcal{M}$). To see why this is the case, let S, T be instances of $\mathbf{R_1}$ and $\mathbf{R_2}$, respectively, such that:

$$E^S \;\; = \;\; \{(1,2),(2,3)\} \qquad\qquad F^T \;\; = \;\; \{(1,3)\}$$
$$G^T \;\; = \;\; \{4\}$$

It is clear that $(S,T) \notin \mathcal{M}$ as element 2 is not in G^T. However, $(S,T) \in \mathcal{M} \circ \mathcal{M}_1 \circ \mathcal{M}$ since for the instances T_1, S_1 of $\mathbf{R_2}$ and $\mathbf{R_1}$, respectively, such that:

$$F^{T_1} \;\; = \;\; \{(1,3)\} \qquad\qquad E^{S_1} \;\; = \;\; \{(1,4),(4,3)\}$$
$$G^{T_1} \;\; = \;\; \{2\}$$

we have that $(S,T_1) \in \mathcal{M}$, $(T_1,S_1) \in \mathcal{M}_1$ and $(S_1,T) \in \mathcal{M}$. Thus, we conclude that $\mathcal{M}_1$ does not satisfy condition (2) in Proposition 3.26, from which we conclude that $\mathcal{M}_1$ is not a maximum recovery of $\mathcal{M}$.   □

As we pointed out before, the main motivation for the introduction of the notion of maximum recovery is to have an inverse operator that is defined for every mapping specified by st-tgds. Here, we identify the class of mappings for which this operator is defined by providing a necessary and sufficient condition for the existence of maximum recoveries. In particular, we use this condition to show that every mapping specified by a finite set of st-tgds admits a maximum recovery.

Recall that in Section 3.3.1, we introduced the notion of a strong witness to characterize Fagin-invertibility for the class of total and closed-down on the left mappings. Given a mapping $\mathcal{M}$ from a schema $\mathbf{R_1}$ to a schema $\mathbf{R_2}$ and instances S,T of $\mathbf{R_1}$ and $\mathbf{R_2}$, respectively, T is a strong witness for S under $\mathcal{M}$ if for every instance S' of $\mathbf{R_1}$ such that $T \in \mathrm{Sol}_{\mathcal{M}}(S')$, it holds that $S' \subseteq S$. It turns out that by weakening this condition, one can characterize the existence of maximum recoveries.

Given a mapping $\mathcal{M}$ from a schema $\mathbf{R_1}$ to a schema $\mathbf{R_2}$ and instances S, T of $\mathbf{R_1}$ and $\mathbf{R_2}$, respectively, T is a *witness* for S under $\mathcal{M}$ if for every instance S' of $\mathbf{R_1}$ such that $T \in \mathrm{Sol}_{\mathcal{M}}(S')$, it holds that $\mathrm{Sol}_{\mathcal{M}}(S) \subseteq \mathrm{Sol}_{\mathcal{M}}(S')$. Moreover, T is a witness solution for S under $\mathcal{M}$ if T is both a solution and a witness for S under $\mathcal{M}$.

The notion of a witness is indeed weaker than the notion of a strong witness as the next result shows.

Proposition 3.28   *Let $\mathcal{M} = (\mathbf{R_1}, \mathbf{R_2}, \Sigma)$ be a mapping, where Σ is a finite set of st-tgds, and S an instance of $\mathbf{R_1}$. Then every strong witness for S under $\mathcal{M}$ is a witness for S under $\mathcal{M}$.*

Proof. The proposition is a corollary of the fact that if $\mathcal{M} = (\mathbf{R_1}, \mathbf{R_2}, \Sigma)$, with Σ a set of st-tgds, and S_1, S_2 are instances of $\mathbf{R_1}$ such that $S_1 \subseteq S_2$, then $\mathrm{Sol}_{\mathcal{M}}(S_2) \subseteq \mathrm{Sol}_{\mathcal{M}}(S_1)$.   □

Proposition 3.29   *Let $\mathcal{M} = (\mathbf{R_1}, \mathbf{R_2}, \Sigma)$ be a mapping, where Σ is a finite set of st-tgds, and S an instance of $\mathbf{R_1}$. If T is a universal solution for S under $\mathcal{M}$, then T is a witness solution for S under $\mathcal{M}$.*

Proof. In the proof of Proposition 3.19, we show that if T is a universal solution for S under $\mathcal{M}$ and $T \in \text{SOL}_{\mathcal{M}}(S')$, then $\text{SOL}_{\mathcal{M}}(S) \subseteq \text{SOL}_{\mathcal{M}}(S')$ (this is a corollary of the fact that a mapping specified by a finite set of st-tgds is closed under target homomorphisms). Thus, we have already provided a proof of the proposition. □

We now show that the notion of witness solution can be used to characterize the existence of maximum recoveries.

Theorem 3.30   *Let $\mathcal{M}$ be a mapping from a schema $\mathbf{R_1}$ to a schema $\mathbf{R_2}$. Then $\mathcal{M}$ has a maximum recovery if and only if every instance $S \in \text{DOM}(\mathcal{M})$ has a witness solution under $\mathcal{M}$.*

Proof. ($\Rightarrow$) Let $\mathcal{M}'$ be a maximum recovery of $\mathcal{M}$, and S an instance in $\text{DOM}(\mathcal{M})$. Then given that $\mathcal{M}'$ is a recovery of $\mathcal{M}$, we have that there exists an instance T of $\mathbf{R_2}$ such that $(S, T) \in \mathcal{M}$ and $(T, S) \in \mathcal{M}'$. Next, we show that T is a witness solution for S under $\mathcal{M}$. We already know that T is a solution for S under $\mathcal{M}$, so we only need to show that if $T \in \text{SOL}_{\mathcal{M}}(S')$, then it holds that $\text{SOL}_{\mathcal{M}}(S) \subseteq \text{SOL}_{\mathcal{M}}(S')$. Then assume that $T' \in \text{SOL}_{\mathcal{M}}(S)$. Given that $(S', T) \in \mathcal{M}$, $(T, S) \in \mathcal{M}'$ and $(S, T') \in \mathcal{M}$, we have that $(S', T') \in \mathcal{M} \circ \mathcal{M}' \circ \mathcal{M}$. But from Proposition 3.26, we have that $\mathcal{M} = \mathcal{M} \circ \mathcal{M}' \circ \mathcal{M}$, and, therefore, $(S', T') \in \mathcal{M}$. We conclude that $\text{SOL}_{\mathcal{M}}(S) \subseteq \text{SOL}_{\mathcal{M}}(S')$, and, hence, T is a witness solution for S under $\mathcal{M}$.

($\Leftarrow$) Assume that every $S \in \text{DOM}(\mathcal{M})$ has a witness solution under $\mathcal{M}$, and let $\mathcal{M}^\star$ be a mapping from $\mathbf{R_2}$ to $\mathbf{R_1}$ defined as:

$$\{(T, S) \mid T \text{ is a witness solution for } S \text{ under } \mathcal{M}\}.$$

By hypothesis, we have that $\mathcal{M}^\star$ is a recovery of $\mathcal{M}$. Next, we use Proposition 3.26 to show that $\mathcal{M}^\star$ is a maximum recovery of $\mathcal{M}$.

By definition of $\mathcal{M}^\star$, we have that this mappings satisfies condition (1) in Proposition 3.26. Moreover, given that $\mathcal{M}^\star$ is a recovery of $\mathcal{M}$, we have that $\mathcal{M} \subseteq \mathcal{M} \circ \mathcal{M}^\star \circ \mathcal{M}$. Thus, we have from Proposition 3.26 that if $\mathcal{M} \circ \mathcal{M}^\star \circ \mathcal{M} \subseteq \mathcal{M}$, then $\mathcal{M}^\star$ is a maximum recovery of $\mathcal{M}$. Let $(S, T) \in \mathcal{M} \circ \mathcal{M}^\star \circ \mathcal{M}$. Then there exist instances T_1, S_1 of $\mathbf{R_2}$ and $\mathbf{R_1}$, respectively, such that $(S, T_1) \in \mathcal{M}$, $(T_1, S_1) \in \mathcal{M}^\star$ and $(S_1, T) \in \mathcal{M}$. Thus, by definition of $\mathcal{M}^\star$, we have that T_1 is a witness solution for S_1 under $\mathcal{M}$. Hence, given that $T_1 \in \text{SOL}_{\mathcal{M}}(S)$, we have that $\text{SOL}_{\mathcal{M}}(S_1) \subseteq \text{SOL}_{\mathcal{M}}(S)$. We conclude that $T \in \text{SOL}_{\mathcal{M}}(S)$ since $T \in \text{SOL}_{\mathcal{M}}(S_1)$, and, thus, we have that $(S, T) \in \mathcal{M}$, which was to be shown. This concludes the proof of the theorem. □

As a corollary of Proposition 3.29 and Theorem 3.30, we obtain the desired result that every mapping specified by a finite set of st-tgds admits a maximum recovery. It should be noticed that this result is in sharp contrast with the non-existence result for the notion of Fagin-inverse for the class of mappings specified by st-tgds (see Corollary 3.16).

Theorem 3.31   *Every mapping specified by a finite set of st-tgds admits a maximum recovery.*

Up to this point, we have introduced two alternative inverse operators for schema mappings: Fagin-inverses and maximum recoveries. Thus, it is natural to ask what is the relationship between these concepts. We now show that for the class of mappings for which the notion of Fagin-inverse is appropriate, the notion of maximum recovery strictly generalizes the notion of Fagin-inverse.

Proposition 3.32

(1) *There exists a mapping specified by a finite set of st-tgds that is not Fagin-invertible but has a maximum recovery.*

(2) *For every total, closed-down on the left and Fagin-invertible mapping $\mathcal{M}$, a mapping $\mathcal{M}'$ is a Fagin-inverse of $\mathcal{M}$ if and only if $\mathcal{M}'$ is a maximum recovery of $\mathcal{M}$.*

Proof. Part (1) is a consequence of Corollary 3.16 and Theorem 3.31. Part (2) is left as an exercise for the reader.   □

Given that Fagin-inverses are not guaranteed to exist for the class of mappings specified by st-tgds, we studied in Section 3.3.1 the decidability of Fagin-invertibility for this type of mappings. On the other hand, the problem of checking whether a mapping $\mathcal{M}$ has a maximum recovery becomes trivial in this context, as every mapping specified by this type of dependencies admits a maximum recovery. Thus, we only consider here the problem of checking, given mappings $\mathcal{M}$ and $\mathcal{M}'$ specified by st-tgds, whether $\mathcal{M}'$ is a maximum recovery of $\mathcal{M}$. Somewhat surprisingly, not only is this problem undecidable, but also so is the problem of checking whether a mapping $\mathcal{M}'$ is a recovery of a mapping $\mathcal{M}$.

Theorem 3.33   *The problem of checking, given mappings $\mathcal{M} = (\mathbf{R_1}, \mathbf{R_2}, \Sigma_{12})$ and $\mathcal{M}' = (\mathbf{R_2}, \mathbf{R_1}, \Sigma_{21})$ with Σ_{12} and Σ_{21} finite sets of st-tgds, whether $\mathcal{M}'$ is a recovery (maximum recovery) of $\mathcal{M}$ is undecidable.*

As we have mentioned in the previous sections, we are still missing the algorithms for computing the inverse operators introduced in this chapter. In the next section, we present a unified algorithm for computing these operators, which uses some query rewriting techniques and takes advantage of the tight connection between the notions of Fagin-inverse and maximum recovery shown in Proposition 3.32.

3.3.3   COMPUTING THE INVERSE OPERATOR

Up to this point, we have introduced and compared two notions of inverse proposed in the literature, focusing mainly on the problem of the existence of such inverses. Arguably, the most important problem about these operators is the issue of how to compute them for the class of mappings specified by st-tgds. In this section, we present an algorithm for computing maximum recoveries of mappings specified by st-tgds, which by the results of the previous sections can also be used to compute Fagin-inverses for this type of mappings. Interestingly, this algorithm is based on *query rewriting*, which greatly simplifies the process of computing such inverses.

We start by recalling the definition of query rewritability over the source from Section 2.4.2. Let M be a mapping from a schema $\mathbf{R}_1$ to a schema $\mathbf{R}_2$ and Q a query over schema $\mathbf{R}_2$. Then a query Q' is said to be a *rewriting of Q over the source* if Q' is a query over $\mathbf{R}_1$ such that for every $S \in \text{INST}(\mathbf{R}_1)$, it holds that $Q'(S) = certain_M(Q, S)$. That is, it is possible to obtain the set of certain answers of Q over S under M by just evaluating its rewriting Q' over the source S.

The computation of a source rewriting of a conjunctive query is a basic step in the algorithm presented in this section. This problem has been extensively studied in the database area and, in particular, in the data integration context. In fact, it is well known that:

Proposition 3.34   *There exists an algorithm QUERYREWRITING that, given a mapping $M = (\mathbf{R}_1, \mathbf{R}_2, \Sigma)$, with Σ a finite set of st-tgds, and a conjunctive query Q over $\mathbf{R}_2$, computes a union of conjunctive queries with equality Q' that is a rewriting of Q over the source. The algorithm runs in exponential time and its output is of exponential size in the size of Σ and Q.*

Example 3.35   We give here some intuition of why the algorithm QUERYREWRITING uses union and equalities in its output language. Let $\mathbf{R}_1$ be a schema consisting of a unary relation P and a binary relation R, $\mathbf{R}_2$ be a schema consisting of a binary relation T and $M = (\mathbf{R}_1, \mathbf{R}_2, \Sigma)$, where Σ is a set of dependencies consisting of the following st-tgds:

$$
\begin{aligned}
P(x) &\rightarrow T(x, x), \\
R(x, y) &\rightarrow T(x, y).
\end{aligned}
$$

Assume that Q is the target query $T(x, y)$. What is a source rewriting of Q? To answer this question, we need to consider all the possible ways of generating target tuples from a source instance. Let S be an instance of $\mathbf{R}_1$. If S contains a fact $P(a)$, then all the solutions for S under M will contain the fact $T(a, a)$. Thus, every answer to the query $P(x) \wedge x = y$ over S will be in $certain_M(Q, S)$. In the same way, if S contains a fact $R(a, b)$, then all the solutions for S under M will contain the fact $T(a, b)$ and, hence, every answer to the query $R(x, y)$ over S will be in $certain_M(Q, S)$. Given the definition of M, the previous two queries consider all the possible ways to generate target tuples according to M, from which one can formally prove that the following is a source rewriting of query Q:

$$(P(x) \wedge x = y) \vee R(x, y).$$

It is important to notice that the above query is a union of two conjunctive queries, and that the use of union and equality in this rewriting is unavoidable.   □

We finally have all the necessary ingredients to present the algorithm for computing maximum recoveries. In this procedure, $\mathbf{C}$ refers to the unary predicate introduced in Section 2 that distinguishes between constant and null values ($\mathbf{C}(a)$ holds if and only if a belongs to Const). Moreover, if $\bar{x} = (x_1, \ldots, x_k)$, then $\mathbf{C}(\bar{x})$ is used in the algorithm as a shorthand for $\mathbf{C}(x_1) \wedge \cdots \wedge \mathbf{C}(x_k)$.

Algorithm 3 MAXIMUMRECOVERY

Require: $\mathcal{M}_{12} = (\mathbf{R_1}, \mathbf{R_2}, \Sigma)$ with Σ a finite set of st-tgds
Ensure: $\mathcal{M}_{21} = (\mathbf{R_2}, \mathbf{R_1}, \Gamma)$ is a maximum recovery of $\mathcal{M}$
 1: $\Gamma := \emptyset$
 2: **for all** $\varphi(\bar{x}) \rightarrow \exists \bar{y}\, \psi(\bar{x}, \bar{y})$ in Σ **do**
 3:     $Q(\bar{x}) := \exists \bar{y}\, \psi(\bar{x}, \bar{y})$
 4:     let $\alpha(\bar{x})$ be the output of algorithm QUERYREWRITING with input $\mathcal{M}_{12}$ and Q
 5:     $\Gamma := \Gamma \cup \{\psi(\bar{x}, \bar{y}) \wedge \mathbf{C}(\bar{x}) \rightarrow \alpha(\bar{x})\}$
 6: **end for**

Theorem 3.36 *Algorithm* MAXIMUMRECOVERY *runs in exponential time, and on input* $\mathcal{M} = (\mathbf{R_1}, \mathbf{R_2}, \Sigma)$, *where* Σ *is a finite set of st-tgds, it computes a maximum recovery of* $\mathcal{M}$.

Proof. From Proposition 3.34, it is straightforward to conclude that algorithm MAXIMUMRECOVERY runs in exponential time. Assume that $\mathcal{M}' = (\mathbf{R_1}, \mathbf{R_2}, \Gamma)$ is the output of the algorithm MAXIMUMRECOVERY with input $\mathcal{M}$. In order to prove that $\mathcal{M}'$ is a maximum recovery of $\mathcal{M}$, we first show that $\mathcal{M}'$ is a recovery of $\mathcal{M}$, that is, we prove that for every instance S of $\mathbf{R_1}$, it holds that $(S, S) \in \mathcal{M} \circ \mathcal{M}'$.

Let S be an instance of $\mathbf{R_1}$ and let T be the canonical universal solution for S under $\mathcal{M}$. Next, we show that $(T, S) \in \mathcal{M}'$, from which we conclude that $(S, S) \in \mathcal{M} \circ \mathcal{M}'$ since $(S, T) \in \mathcal{M}$. Let $\sigma \in \Gamma$. We need to show that $(T, S) \models \sigma$. Assume that σ is of the form $\psi(\bar{x}, \bar{y}) \wedge \mathbf{C}(\bar{x}) \rightarrow \alpha(\bar{x})$, and that $\bar{a}$ is a tuple of values from T such that $T \models \exists \bar{y}\, (\psi(\bar{a}, \bar{y}) \wedge \mathbf{C}(\bar{a}))$. We need to show that $S \models \alpha(\bar{a})$. Consider the conjunctive query $Q(\bar{x})$ defined by formula $\exists \bar{y}\, \psi(\bar{x}, \bar{y})$. Since $\mathbf{C}(\bar{a})$ holds and $T \models \exists \bar{y}\, \psi(\bar{a}, \bar{y})$, we obtain that $\bar{a} \in Q(T)$. Thus, from the results about query answering proved in Section 2.4 and the fact that T is the canonical universal solution for S under $\mathcal{M}$, we obtain that $\bar{a} \in certain_{\mathcal{M}}(Q, S)$. Consider now the query $Q'(\bar{x})$ defined by formula $\alpha(\bar{x})$. By the definition of algorithm MAXIMUMRECOVERY, we have that Q' is a rewriting of Q over schema $\mathbf{R_1}$, and then $certain_{\mathcal{M}}(Q, S) = Q'(S)$. Thus, we have that $\bar{a} \in Q'(S)$, and then $S \models \alpha(\bar{a})$, which was to be shown.

Given that $\mathcal{M}'$ is a recovery of $\mathcal{M}$ and $\text{DOM}(\mathcal{M}) = \text{INST}(\mathbf{R_1})$, we know from Proposition 3.26 that $\mathcal{M}'$ is a maximum recovery of $\mathcal{M}$ if $\mathcal{M} \circ \mathcal{M}' \circ \mathcal{M} \subseteq \mathcal{M}$. Next, we show that if $(S_1, S_2) \in \mathcal{M} \circ \mathcal{M}'$, then $\text{SOL}_{\mathcal{M}}(S_2) \subseteq \text{SOL}_{\mathcal{M}}(S_1)$, from which we conclude that $\mathcal{M} \circ \mathcal{M}' \circ \mathcal{M} \subseteq \mathcal{M}$. To see why this is the case, let $(S, T) \in \mathcal{M} \circ \mathcal{M}' \circ \mathcal{M}$. Then there exist instances T_1, R_1 of $\mathbf{R_2}$ and $\mathbf{R_1}$, respectively, such that $(S, T_1) \in \mathcal{M}$, $(T_1, S_1) \in \mathcal{M}'$ and $(S_1, T) \in \mathcal{M}$. Then given that $(S, S_1) \in$

$\mathcal{M} \circ \mathcal{M}'$, we have by hypothesis that $\text{SOL}_{\mathcal{M}}(S_1) \subseteq \text{SOL}_{\mathcal{M}}(S)$. Thus, from the fact that $(S_1, T) \in \mathcal{M}$, we conclude that $(S, T) \in \mathcal{M}$, which was to be shown.

Let $(S_1, S_2) \in \mathcal{M} \circ \mathcal{M}'$, and $T^{\star}$ an instance of $\mathbf{R_2}$ such that $(S_1, T^{\star}) \in \mathcal{M}$ and $(T^{\star}, S_2) \in \mathcal{M}'$. We need to prove that $\text{SOL}_{\mathcal{M}}(S_2) \subseteq \text{SOL}_{\mathcal{M}}(S_1)$. To this end, assume that $T \in \text{SOL}_{\mathcal{M}}(S_2)$. Next, we show that $T \in \text{SOL}_{\mathcal{M}}(S_1)$. Let $\sigma \in \Sigma$ be a dependency of the form $\varphi(\bar{x}) \rightarrow \exists \bar{y} \, \psi(\bar{x}, \bar{y})$, and assume that $S_1 \models \varphi(\bar{a})$ for some tuple $\bar{a}$ of constant values. We show next that $T \models \exists \bar{y} \, \psi(\bar{a}, \bar{y})$. Given that $S_1 \models \varphi(\bar{a})$, we have that for every $T' \in \text{SOL}_{\mathcal{M}}(S_1)$, it holds that $T' \models \exists \bar{y} \, \psi(\bar{a}, \bar{y})$. In particular, it holds that $T^{\star} \models \exists \bar{y} \, \psi(\bar{a}, \bar{y})$. By the definition of algorithm MAXIMUMRECOVERY, we know that there exists a dependency $\psi(\bar{x}, \bar{y}) \wedge \mathbf{C}(\bar{x}) \rightarrow \alpha(\bar{x})$ in Γ such that $\alpha(\bar{x})$ is a rewriting of $\exists \bar{y} \, \psi(\bar{x}, \bar{y})$ over $\mathbf{R_1}$. Then since $T^{\star} \models \exists \bar{y} \, \psi(\bar{a}, \bar{y})$, $\bar{a}$ is a tuple of constant values, and $(T^{\star}, S_2) \models \Gamma$, we know that $S_2 \models \alpha(\bar{a})$. Now consider the queries $Q(\bar{x})$ and $Q'(\bar{x})$ defined by formulas $\exists \bar{y} \, \psi(\bar{x}, \bar{y})$ and $\alpha(\bar{x})$, respectively. Since $S_2 \models \alpha(\bar{a})$, we know that $\bar{a} \in Q'(S_2)$. Furthermore, we know that $Q'(S_2) = \textit{certain}_{\mathcal{M}}(Q, S_2)$, and then $\bar{a} \in \textit{certain}_{\mathcal{M}}(Q, S_2)$. In particular, since $T \in \text{SOL}_{\mathcal{M}}(S_2)$, we know that $\bar{a} \in Q(T)$, from which we conclude that $T \models \exists \bar{y} \, \psi(\bar{a}, \bar{y})$. We have shown that for every $\sigma \in \Sigma$ of the form $\varphi(\bar{x}) \rightarrow \exists \bar{y} \, \psi(\bar{x}, \bar{y})$, if $S_1 \models \varphi(\bar{a})$ for some tuple $\bar{a}$, then $T \models \exists \bar{y} \, \psi(\bar{a}, \bar{y})$. Thus, we have that $(S_1, T) \models \Sigma$, and, therefore, $T \in \text{SOL}_{\mathcal{M}}(S_1)$. This concludes the proof of the theorem. $\square$

Example 3.37   Let $\mathbf{R_1}$ be a schema consisting of a unary relation P and a binary relation R, $\mathbf{R_2}$ be a schema consisting of a binary relation T and $\mathcal{M} = (\mathbf{R_1}, \mathbf{R_2}, \Sigma)$, where Σ is a set of dependencies consisting of the following st-tgds:

$$\begin{aligned} P(x) &\rightarrow T(x, x), \\ R(x, y) &\rightarrow T(x, y). \end{aligned}$$

In order to compute a maximum recovery $\mathcal{M}' = (\mathbf{R_2}, \mathbf{R_1}, \Gamma)$ of $\mathcal{M}$, algorithm MAXIMUMRECOVERY first computes a source rewriting of target query $T(x, x)$:

$$P(x) \vee R(x, x),$$

and it adds dependency

$$T(x, x) \wedge \mathbf{C}(x) \quad \rightarrow \quad P(x) \vee R(x, x) \tag{3.13}$$

to Γ. Then it computes a rewriting of target query $T(x, y)$ (see Example 3.35):

$$(P(x) \wedge x = y) \vee R(x, y),$$

and it finishes by adding dependency

$$T(x, y) \wedge \mathbf{C}(x) \wedge \mathbf{C}(y) \quad \rightarrow \quad (P(x) \wedge x = y) \vee R(x, y) \tag{3.14}$$

to Γ. Given that (3.14) logically implies (3.13), we conclude that the mapping specified by dependency (3.14) is a maximum recovery of $\mathcal{M}$. $\square$

From Theorem 3.36 and Proposition 3.32, we conclude that algorithm MAXIMUMRECOVERY can also be used to compute Fagin-inverses.

Corollary 3.38 *Let $\mathcal{M} = (\mathbf{R_1}, \mathbf{R_2}, \Sigma)$, where Σ is a finite set of st-tgds. If $\mathcal{M}$ is Fagin-invertible, then on input $\mathcal{M}$, algorithm MAXIMUMRECOVERY computes a Fagin-inverse of $\mathcal{M}$.*

One of the interesting features of algorithm MAXIMUMRECOVERY is the use of query rewriting, as it allows one to reuse in the computation of the inverse operator the large number of techniques developed to deal with the problem of query rewriting. However, one can identify one drawback in this procedure. Algorithm MAXIMUMRECOVERY returns mappings that are specified by dependencies that extend st-tgds with disjunctions in the right-hand side. Unfortunately, this type of mappings are difficult to use in the data exchange context. In particular, it is not clear whether the standard chase procedure could be used to produce a single canonical target database in this case, thus making the process of exchanging data and answering target queries much more complicated. Therefore, it is natural to ask whether the use of disjunction in the output language of algorithm MAXIMUMRECOVERY can be avoided and, in particular, whether the maximum recovery of a mapping specified by st-tgds can be specified in the same mapping language. We conclude this section by giving a negative answer to this question not only for the notion of maximum recovery but also for the notion of Fagin-inverse.

Proposition 3.39 *There exists a mapping $\mathcal{M} = (\mathbf{R_1}, \mathbf{R_2}, \Sigma)$ specified by a finite set Σ of st-tgds that is Fagin-invertible but has no Fagin-inverse specified by a finite set of tgds.*

Proof. Let $\mathbf{R_1}$ be a schema consisting of a unary predicate A and a binary predicate B, $\mathbf{R_2}$ a schema consisting of unary predicates D, E and a binary predicate F, and Σ a set consisting of the following st-tgds:

$$
\begin{aligned}
A(x) &\rightarrow D(x), \\
A(x) &\rightarrow F(x, x), \\
B(x, y) &\rightarrow F(x, y), \\
B(x, x) &\rightarrow E(x).
\end{aligned}
$$

It is possible to prove that $\mathcal{M}$ is Fagin-invertible but has no Fagin-inverse specified by a finite set of tgds. □

Proposition 3.39 shows that the language of tgds is not closed under the notion of Fagin-inverse. By combining this result with Proposition 3.32, we conclude that the same holds for the notion of maximum recovery.

Corollary 3.40 *There exists a mapping $\mathcal{M} = (\mathbf{R_1}, \mathbf{R_2}, \Sigma)$ specified by a finite set Σ of st-tgds that has no maximum recovery specified by a finite set of tgds.*

3.4   SUMMARY

- The semantics of the composition operator for schema mappings can be defined as the usual composition of binary relations.

- There exist two mappings specified by finite sets of st-tgds whose composition is not even definable in first-order logic, let alone by st-tgds.

- The language of second-order tuple-generating dependencies is the right language for handling the composition of mappings. First, it is closed under composition. Second, every mapping from this class arises as the composition of several mappings based on st-tgds.

- The key issue in the study of the inverse operator for schema mappings is to provide a good semantics for it.

- A mapping $\mathcal{M}'$ is a Fagin-inverse of a mapping $\mathcal{M}$ if the composition of $\mathcal{M}$ with $\mathcal{M}'$ is equal to the identity mapping. There exists a mapping specified by a finite set of st-tgds that does not admit a Fagin-inverse.

- The main goal behind the notion of recovery is to give a formal definition for what it means for a mapping $\mathcal{M}'$ to recover sound information with respect to a mapping $\mathcal{M}$. A maximum recovery is a recovery that brings back the maximum amount of sound information.

- The notions of recovery and maximum recovery were introduced to overcome some of the limitations of Fagin-inverses. In particular, every mapping specified by a finite set of st-tgds admits a maximum recovery.

3.5   BIBLIOGRAPHIC COMMENTS

The composition operator for schema mappings has been extensively studied [Arenas et al., 2009b, 2010; Bernstein, 2003; Bernstein et al., 2008; Fagin et al., 2005c; Libkin and Sirangelo, 2008; Madhavan and Halevy, 2003; Nash et al., 2007; Yu and Popa, 2005]. The semantics of the composition presented in Section 3.2 was introduced by Fagin et al. [2005c]. The authors have shown that the composition problem is NP-complete; from this it follows that there exist mappings specified by st-tgds whose composition cannot be expressed in first-order logic. Fagin et al. [2005c] propose the language of second-order tuple-generating dependencies (SO tgds) and study its basic properties.

The notion of Fagin-inverse was proposed by Fagin [2007]. Fagin called it just an inverse as it was the first notion of an inverse of a schema mapping. We reserve the term *inverse* to refer to the general operator and use the name *Fagin-inverse* for the notion proposed by Fagin [2007]. The problem of existence of Fagin-inverses was also studied by Fagin et al. [2008] and Arenas et al. [2009d]. Complexity issues related to the notion of Fagin-inverse were studied by Arenas et al. [2009d]; Fagin [2007]; Fagin and Nash [2010].

The notions of recovery and maximum recovery were proposed by Arenas et al. [2009d]. The authors proved the necessary and sufficient condition for the existence of maximum recoveries given in this chapter and showed that every mapping specified by a finite set of st-tgds admits a maximum recovery. They also established the tight connection between the notions of Fagin-inverse and maximum recovery. The algorithm for computing Fagin-inverses and maximum recoveries presented in this chapter was proposed by Arenas et al. [2009c,d]. Finally, results about languages needed to express Fagin-inverses and maximum recoveries were given by Fagin et al. [2008] and Arenas et al. [2009d], respectively.

CHAPTER 4

XML Mappings and Data Exchange

4.1 XML DATABASES

We begin this chapter by introducing formally an abstract model of XML databases. In this model, data are organized into trees, and queries are expressed with patterns. Compared to the relational model, the tree model gives more opportunities for expressing structural properties of data even with simple queries based on patterns. On the other hand, schemas impose strong conditions on the structure of source and target instances, entering into complex interactions with source-to-target dependencies, which makes consistency one of the central issues in XML data exchange.

4.1.1 XML DOCUMENTS AND DTDS

Just as relations are abstractions of tables, trees are abstractions of XML documents. Let us look at a concrete example, shown in Fig. 4.2. In this tree, `europe`, `country`, and `ruler` are node labels. They come from a finite labeling alphabet and correspond to relation names from the classical setting. The values given in parentheses are so called *data values*, and they come from a possibly infinite set (in our example, the set of strings over a finite alphabet). Thus each `country`-node and each `ruler`-node has an *attribute* that stores a data value.

Formally, we view XML documents over a labeling alphabet Γ of *element types* and a set of attributes *Att* as structures

$$T = \langle U, \downarrow, \rightarrow, lab, (\rho_a)_{a \in Att} \rangle,$$

where

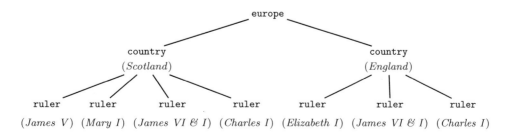

Figure 4.1: An XML tree.

- U is an unranked tree domain: that is, a finite subset of $\mathbb{N}^*$ (the set of strings of natural numbers) that is prefix-closed, and if $n \cdot i \in U$, then $n \cdot j \in U$ for all $j < i$ (these strings are nodes of a tree: if n is a node tree with m children, then those children are represented by the strings $n \cdot 0, \ldots, n \cdot (m - 1)$);

- the binary relations $\downarrow$ and $\rightarrow$ are the child relation ($n \downarrow n \cdot i$) and the next sibling relation ($n \cdot i \rightarrow n \cdot (i + 1)$);

- $lab : U \rightarrow \Gamma$ is the labeling function; and

- each ρ_a is a partial function from U to $\texttt{Const}$, the domain of attribute values, that gives the values of a for all the nodes in U where it is defined.

A DTD D over Γ with a distinguished symbol r (for the root) and a set of attributes Att consists of a mapping P_D from Γ to regular expressions over $\Gamma - \{r\}$ (one typically writes them as productions $\ell \rightarrow e$ if $P_D(\ell) = e$), and a mapping $A_D : \Gamma \rightarrow 2^{Att}$ that assigns a (possibly empty) set of attributes to each element type. We always assume, for notational convenience, that attributes come in some order, just like in the relational case: attributes in tuples come in some order so we can write $R(a_1, \ldots, a_n)$. Likewise, we shall describe an ℓ-labeled tree node with n attributes as $\ell(a_1, \ldots, a_n)$.

A tree T conforms to a DTD D (written as $T \models D$) if its root is labeled r, the set of attributes for a node labeled ℓ is $A_D(\ell)$, and the labels of the children of such a node, read left-to-right, form a string in the language of $P_D(\ell)$.

For example the tree from Fig. 4.1 conforms to the following DTD D_1

$$
\begin{aligned}
\texttt{europe} &\rightarrow \texttt{country}^* &\quad \texttt{country} &: \texttt{@name} \\
\texttt{country} &\rightarrow \texttt{ruler}^* &\quad \texttt{ruler} &: \texttt{@name}
\end{aligned}
$$

where the left column lists the mapping P_D, and the right column lists the mapping A_D. By convention we omit ε-productions on the left, and empty sets on the right.

We shall also refer to a class of *nested-relational DTDs*; as the name suggests, they generalize nested relations. In such DTDs, all productions are of the form $\ell \rightarrow \hat{\ell}_1 \ldots \hat{\ell}_m$, where all ℓ_i's are distinct labels from Γ and $\hat{\ell}_i$ is either ℓ_i or ℓ_i^* or ℓ_i^+ or $\ell_i? = \ell_i | \varepsilon$. Moreover, such DTDs are not recursive, i.e., the graph in which we put an edge between ℓ and all the ℓ_i's for each production has no cycles. An example of a nested-relational DTD is D_1 considered above.

Nested-relational DTDs are very common in practice: some empirical studies suggest that they cover about 70% of real-world DTDs. As we will see shortly, many computational problems become easier for them.

4.1.2 EXPRESSING PROPERTIES OF TREES

Let us return to the example from Fig. 4.1. Observe that information is represented by means of data values, as well as the structure of the tree. For instance, the edge between the node storing *Scotland* and the node storing *Mary I* represents the fact that Mary I ruled Scotland. The value *Charles I* appearing twice informs us that Charles I ruled both Scotland and England. The node storing *Mary I* coming directly after the node storing *James V* corresponds to the fact that Mary I succeeded James V on the throne of Scotland. This already suggests the querying features we need to extract information from XML trees: *child*, *next sibling*, and their transitive closures: *descendant*, *following sibling*. It is also necessary to compare data values stored in different nodes.

Given the developments of the preceding chapters, a natural query language for XML trees is the family of conjunctive queries over XML trees viewed as databases over two sorts of objects: tree nodes and data values. Relations in such representations include child, next sibling, and relations associating attribute values with nodes.

To avoid the syntactically unpleasant formalism of two-sorted structures, conjunctive queries on trees are best formalized by means of tree patterns with variables for attribute values. Nodes are described by formulae $\ell(\bar{x})$, where ℓ is either a label or the wildcard _, and $\bar{x}$ is a tuple of variables corresponding to the attributes of the node. For each node a list of its children and descendants is specified, together with (partial) information on their order.

Formally, tree patterns are given by the following grammar:

$$
\begin{array}{rcll}
\pi & := & \ell(\bar{x})[\lambda] & \text{patterns} \\
\lambda & := & \varepsilon \mid \mu \mid //\pi \mid \lambda, \lambda & \text{sets} \\
\mu & := & \pi \mid \pi \to \mu \mid \pi \to^* \mu & \text{sequences}
\end{array}
\tag{4.1}
$$

We shall abbreviate $\ell(\bar{x})[\varepsilon]$ to just $\ell(\bar{x})$, $\ell(\bar{x})[\pi]$ to $\ell(\bar{x})/\pi$, and $\ell(\bar{x})[//\pi]$ to $\ell(\bar{x})//\pi$. We write $\pi(\bar{x})$ to indicate that $\bar{x}$ is the list of variables used in π. For instance,

$$
\begin{aligned}
\pi_1(x) &= \texttt{europe}[//\texttt{ruler}(x)], \\
\pi_2(x, y) &= \texttt{europe}[\texttt{country}[\texttt{ruler}(x) \to \texttt{ruler}(y)]]
\end{aligned}
$$

can be shortly written as

$$
\begin{aligned}
\pi_1(x) &= \texttt{europe}//\texttt{ruler}(x), \\
\pi_2(x, y) &= \texttt{europe}/\texttt{country}[\texttt{ruler}(x) \to \texttt{ruler}(y)].
\end{aligned}
$$

The semantics of patterns is defined by means of the relation $(T, s) \models \pi(\bar{a})$, saying that $\pi(\bar{x})$ is satisfied in a node s of a tree T when its variables $\bar{x}$ are interpreted as $\bar{a}$. It is defined inductively as follows:

$(T, s) \models \ell(\bar{a})$	iff	s is labeled by ℓ (or $\ell = \_$) and $\bar{a}$ is the tuple of attributes of s;
$(T, s) \models \ell(\bar{a})[\lambda_1, \lambda_2]$	iff	$(T, s) \models \ell(\bar{a})[\lambda_1]$ and $(T, s) \models \ell(\bar{a})[\lambda_2]$;
$(T, s) \models \ell(\bar{a})[\mu]$	iff	$(T, s) \models \ell(\bar{a})$ and $(T, s') \models \mu$ for some s' with $s \downarrow s'$;
$(T, s) \models \ell(\bar{a})[//\pi]$	iff	$(T, s) \models \ell(\bar{a})$ and $(T, s') \models \pi$ for some descendant s' of s;
$(T, s) \models \pi \rightarrow \mu$	iff	$(T, s) \models \pi$ and $(T, s') \models \mu$ for some s' with $s \rightarrow s'$;
$(T, s) \models \pi \rightarrow^* \mu$	iff	$(T, s) \models \pi$ and $(T, s') \models \mu$ for some s' with $s \rightarrow^* s'$.

Observe that semantically "sets" in tree patterns are literally sets: for a node satisfying $\ell(\bar{a})[\lambda_1, \lambda_2]$, the nodes witnessing λ_1 are not necessarily distinct from the ones witnessing λ_2.

For a tree T and a pattern π, we write $T \models \pi(\bar{a})$ iff $(T, r) \models \pi(\bar{a})$, that is, patterns are witnessed at the root. This is not a restriction since we have descendant $//$ in the language, and we can thus express satisfaction of a pattern in an arbitrary node of a tree. We also denote the set $\{\bar{a} \mid T \models \pi(\bar{a})\}$ by $\pi(T)$.

If T is the tree from Fig. 4.1,

$$\pi_1(T) = \{\textit{James V, Mary I, James VI \& I, Charles I, Elizabeth I}\},$$
$$\pi_2(T) = \{(\textit{James V, Mary I}), (\textit{Mary I, James VI \& I}), (\textit{James VI \& I, Charles I}),$$
$$(\textit{Elizabeth I, James VI \& I})\}.$$

Observe that the patterns already can express equalities between data values by simply repeating variables. For instance

$$\texttt{europe[country/ruler}(x) \rightarrow^* \texttt{country/ruler}(x)]$$

lists the rulers that ruled more than one country ($\rightarrow^*$ is the transitive closure of $\rightarrow$, not reflexive-transitive). Inequalities have to be added explicitly. To keep the setting uniform, we also allow explicit equalities.

Generalized tree patterns are expressions of the form $\pi(\bar{x}) \wedge \alpha(\bar{x})$, where $\pi(\bar{x})$ is a tree pattern and $\alpha(\bar{x})$ is a conjunction of equalities and inequalities among variables $\bar{x}$. The semantics is naturally extended:

$$T \models \pi(\bar{a}) \wedge \alpha(\bar{a}) \quad \text{iff} \quad T \models \pi(\bar{a}) \text{ and } \alpha(\bar{a}) \text{ holds}.$$

For example the pattern

$$\texttt{europe[country[ruler}(y) \rightarrow \texttt{ruler}(x)], \texttt{country[ruler}(z) \rightarrow \texttt{ruler}(x)]] \wedge y \neq z$$

expresses the fact that x succeeded two different rulers, y and z.

From now on, whenever we write *pattern*, we mean *generalized tree pattern*. The non-generalized tree patterns are referred to as *pure patterns*.

Classification of patterns.   In our analysis, we often consider patterns with a restricted set of available axes and comparisons. We denote classes of patterns by $\Pi(\sigma)$, where σ is a signature indicating which axes and comparisons are present. We refer to the usual navigational axes as $\downarrow$ (child), $\downarrow^*$ (descendant), $\rightarrow$ (next-sibling), $\rightarrow^*$ (following-sibling). Equality and inequality requires some explanation. Having $\neq$ in σ means that we can use conjuncts of the form $x \neq y$ in the patterns; having $=$ in σ means that we can use explicit equalities $x = y$ in patterns, as well as reuse variables. If $=$ is not in σ, we are only allowed to reuse variables in inequalities (if $\neq$ is in σ) or nowhere at all. We also specify if _ (wildcard) can be used or not. If not, only $\ell(\bar{x})$ with $\ell \in \Gamma$ are allowed.

Abbreviations.   To save space, we often write $\Downarrow$ for the pair $(\downarrow, \downarrow^*)$, and $\Rightarrow$ for the pair $(\rightarrow, \rightarrow^*)$.

A pure tree pattern can be seen as a tree-like structure

$$S_\pi = \langle U, \downarrow, \downarrow^*, \rightarrow, \rightarrow^*, lab, \pi, \rho \rangle,$$

where U is the set of (occurrences of) sub-patterns of π of the form $\ell(\bar{x})[\lambda]$, with lab and ρ naturally defined as $lab(\ell(\bar{x})[\lambda]) = \ell$ and $\rho(\ell(\bar{x})[\lambda]) = \bar{x}$. The relation $\downarrow$ contains all pairs $\pi_1, \pi_2 \in U$ such that the set under the head of π_1 contains a list that contains π_2, i.e., $\pi_1 = \ell(\bar{x})[\lambda, \mu \rightsquigarrow \pi_2 \rightsquigarrow \mu', \lambda']$, where $\rightsquigarrow$ is $\rightarrow$ or $\rightarrow^*$, and all $\lambda, \lambda', \mu, \mu'$ can be empty. Similarly, $(\pi_1, \pi_2) \in \downarrow^*$ iff $\pi_1 = \ell(\bar{x})[\lambda, //\pi_2, \lambda']$, $(\pi_1, \pi_2) \in \rightarrow$ iff π contains (syntactically) $\pi_1 \rightarrow \pi_2$, and $(\pi_1, \pi_2) \in \rightarrow^*$ iff π contains $\pi_1 \rightarrow^* \pi_2$.

Under this interpretation, there exists a natural notion of homomorphism. Let $T = \langle U_1, \downarrow, \rightarrow, lab_1, r_1, \rho_1 \rangle$. A homomorphism between π and T is a function that maps U into U_1, and the variables of π into the attribute values of T such that for all $\pi_1, \pi_2 \in U$ the following conditions hold:

1. $h(\pi) = r_1$;
2. if $lab(\pi_1) \neq \_$, then $lab(\pi_1) = lab_1(h(\pi_1))$;
3. if $\pi_1 \downarrow \pi_2$ in S_π, then $h(\pi_1) \downarrow h(\pi_2)$ in T_1;
4. if $\pi_1 \downarrow^* \pi_2$ in S_π, then $h(\pi_1) \downarrow^* h(\pi_2)$ in T_1;
5. if $\pi_1 \rightarrow \pi_2$ in S_π, then $h(\pi_1) \rightarrow h(\pi_2)$ in T_1;
6. if $\pi_1 \rightarrow^* \pi_2$ in S_π, then $h(\pi_1) \rightarrow^* h(\pi_2)$ in T_1;
7. if $\rho(\pi_1)$ is not empty sequence, then $h(\rho(\pi_1)) = \rho_1(h(\pi_1))$.

Note that while in T the relations $\downarrow^*$ and $\rightarrow^*$ are externally defined as transitive closures of $\downarrow$ and $\rightarrow$, in S_π, they are built-in relations. In fact, $\downarrow \cap \downarrow^* = \emptyset$ and $\rightarrow \cap \rightarrow^* = \emptyset$, but all four relations can be extended in such a way that the structure becomes a proper tree.

For a generalized pattern $\pi = \pi_0 \wedge \alpha$, a homomorphism from π to T is a homomorphism from π_0 to T such that

1. for every equality $x = y$ in α, $h(x) = h(y)$;

2. for every inequality $x \neq y$ in α, $h(x) \neq h(y)$.

In either case, we write $h : \pi \to T$ instead of the more formal $h : S_\pi \to T$.

An immediate observation is that the semantics of tree pattern satisfaction can be stated in terms of homomorphisms:

Lemma 4.1 $T \models \pi$ *iff there exists a homomorphism from π to T.*

We now look at basic decision problems related with satisfiability and evaluation of patterns. We start with data and combined complexity of evaluating tree patterns. For data complexity, we fix a pattern π, and we want to check for a given tree T and a tuple $\bar{a}$ whether $T \models \pi(\bar{a})$. For combined complexity, the question is the same, but the input includes T, $\bar{a}$ and π.

Since patterns are essentially conjunctive queries over trees, the data complexity is in LOGSPACE (and the bound cannot be lowered in general, since transitive closures of $\downarrow$ and $\to$ may have to be computed). And since they are nicely structured conjunctive queries, the combined complexity is tractable as well. More precisely, we have:

Proposition 4.2   *The data complexity of evaluating tree patterns is* LOGSPACE-*complete, and the combined complexity is in* PTIME.

Proof. Take a tree pattern π, a valuation $\bar{a}$ and a tree T. Checking that $T \models \pi[\bar{a}]$ can be done in PTIME by a bottom up evaluation of the sub-patterns of $\pi[\bar{a}]$. The idea is to annotate each node v with a set $\Phi(v)$ containing the sub-formulae of $\pi[\bar{a}]$ satisfied in v. More precisely, if v is a leaf labeled with σ and storing a tuple $\bar{b}$, let $\Phi(v)$ contain all sub-patterns of $\pi[\bar{a}]$ of the form $\sigma'(\bar{b})$, with $\sigma' \in \{\sigma, \_\}$. If v is an internal node labeled with σ, having children $v_1, v_2, \ldots, v_k$, and storing a tuple b, let $\Phi(v)$ contain all sub-patterns of $\pi[\bar{a}]$ of the form $\sigma'(\bar{b})[\lambda_1, \lambda_2, \ldots, \lambda_p]$ satisfying

- $\sigma' \in \{\sigma, \_\}$,

- for each $\lambda_i = //\pi_1$ there exists a node v_j such that $//\pi_1 \in \Phi(v_j)$ or $\pi_1 \in \varphi(v_j)$,

- for each $\lambda_i = \pi_1 \rightsquigarrow_1 \pi_2 \rightsquigarrow_2 \ldots \rightsquigarrow_{r-1} \pi_r$ there exists a sequence $1 \leq n_1 < n_2 < \ldots < n_r \leq k$ such that $\pi_j \in \Phi(v_{n_j})$, and if $\rightsquigarrow_j = \to$ then $n_{j+1} = n_j + 1$ for all j,

and all sub-patterns of $\pi[\bar{a}]$ of the form $//\pi_1$ satisfying $\pi_1 \in \Phi(v_j)$ or $//\pi_1 \in \Phi(v_j)$ for some j. The answer is "yes" iff $\pi[\bar{a}] \in \Phi(\varepsilon)$, where ε is the root of the tree.

Let us now consider the data-complexity. Tree patterns can be viewed as first order queries over signature extended with descendent and following-sibling, and so can be evaluated in LOGSPACE, provided we can evaluate descendant and following-sibling tests in LOGSPACE. This can be done since the next-sibling relation graph has the out-degree at most one, and for the child relation graph, the same holds if we only reverse edges. LOGSPACE-hardness follows from the hardness of reachability

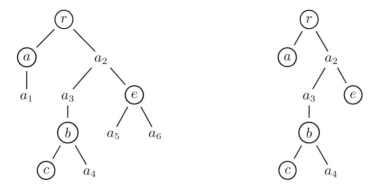

Figure 4.2: A homomorphism from $r[//a, //b/c, //e]$ into a tree and its support.

over successor-relations; hence, even evaluating $r[a \rightarrow^* b]$, over a tree of depth 1, is LOGSPACE-hard.
□

The next problem is the satisfiability for tree patterns. Its input consists of a DTD D and a pattern $\pi(\bar{x})$; the problem is to check whether there is a tree T that conforms to D and has a match for π (i.e., $\pi(T) \neq \emptyset$).

Theorem 4.3 *The satisfiability problem for tree patterns in NP-complete.*

Proof. We shall need the following notion. The *support* of a homomorphism $h : \pi \rightarrow T$, denoted supp h, is the subtree of T obtained by removing all nodes that cannot be reached from range of h by going up, left, and right. For example, consider a tree pattern $r[//a, //b/c, //e]$. This pattern is satisfied by a tree T given in Figure 4.2 with the obvious homomorphism h which appropriately assigns sub-formulae to the encircled nodes. To obtain supp h, we remove all nodes except from ancestors of the nodes from the range of h, and their siblings. The result is shown in Figure 4.2.

Now we show that for each pattern π satisfiable with respect to a DTD D over Γ, there exists a homomorphism from π to some T conforming to D with $\mathcal{O}(\|\pi\| \cdot \|D\|)$ support. Take an arbitrary T conforming to D and satisfying π. Let h be a homomorphism from π to T. Divide the nodes of supp h into four categories: the nodes from the image of h are *red*, the nodes that are not red and have more than one child that is an ancestor of a red node (or is red itself) are *green*, the others are *yellow* if they are ancestors of red nodes, and *blue* otherwise. For example, in Figure 4.2, the encircled nodes are red, a_2 is green, a_3 is yellow, and a_4 is blue. Let N_{red}, N_{green}, N_{yellow}, and N_{blue} be the numbers of red, green, yellow, and blue nodes.

By definition, $N_{\text{red}} \leq \|\pi\|$. Also $N_{\text{green}} \leq \|\pi\|$: when going bottom-up, each green node decreases the number of subtrees containing a red node by at least one, and since we arrive at the root with one subtree containing a red node, $N_{\text{green}} \leq N_{\text{red}}$. By a pumping argument, we may assume that all yellow paths in supp h are not longer than $|\Delta| \leq \|D\|$. Similarly, all blue sequences of siblings in supp h are not longer than the maximal number of states in the automata representing the regular expressions in D, which can also be bounded by $\|D\|$. The number of (maximal) yellow paths is at most $N_{\text{red}} + N_{\text{green}}$. Hence there are at most $2\|\pi\| \cdot \|D\|$ yellow nodes. Since all blue nodes are siblings of nodes of other colors, the number of (maximal) blue sequences of siblings is at most $2(N_{\text{red}} + N_{\text{green}} + N_{\text{yellow}}) \leq 4\|\pi\| \cdot (\|D\| + 1)$ and so $N_{\text{blue}} \leq 4\|\pi\| \cdot (\|D\| + 1)\|D\|$. Altogether, we have at most $2\|\pi\|(\|D\| + 1)(2\|D\| + 1) \leq 12\|\pi\| \cdot \|D\|^2$ nodes.

Now, to decide satisfiability, first guess a polynomial support and a homomorphism. Verifying the homomorphism is polynomial in the size of the formula and the support, hence it is polynomial. Verifying that the support is actually a restriction of a tree conforming to D requires a consistency check, which amounts to checking if a given word is in the language defined by a given regular expression and checking if a regular expression defines a nonempty language (for the labels of yellow nodes). Both these checks can be done in polynomial time.

To get NP-completeness, we do a standard 3CNF SAT reduction. In fact, we only use patterns from $\Pi(\downarrow, \_)$ without variables. Take a formula $\psi = \bigwedge_{j=1}^{k} Z_j^1 \vee Z_j^2 \vee Z_j^3$ with $Z_j^i \in \{x_1, x_2, \ldots, x_n, \bar{x}_1, \bar{x}_2, \ldots, \bar{x}_n\}$. Consider a DTD D

$$r \rightarrow x_1 x_2 \cdots x_n$$
$$x_i \rightarrow \{C_j \mid \exists \ell Z_j^\ell = x_i\} | \{C_j \mid \exists \ell Z_j^\ell = \bar{x}_i\} \qquad\qquad 1 \leq i \leq n$$

over the alphabet $\{x_1, x_2, \ldots, x_n, C_1, C_2, \ldots, C_k\}$. In the second rule, interpret each set as a concatenation of all its elements.

The labels C_j are intended to correspond to $Z_j^1 \vee Z_j^2 \vee Z_j^3$. Each tree conforming to D encodes a valuation of all variables x_i: for each x_i, it stores either all conjuncts made true by assigning 1 to x_i or all conjuncts made true by assigning 0 to x_i.

The satisfiability of ψ is equivalent to the satisfiability of the pattern $r[\_/C_1, \_/C_2, \ldots, \_/C_k]$ with respect to D. $\qquad\qquad\square$

4.2   XML SCHEMA MAPPINGS

XML schema mappings resemble relational mappings. Like before, each mappings consists of a source schema, a target schema, and a set of source-to-target tuple generating dependencies relating the two schemas. In the XML context, relational schemas are naturally replaced by DTDs. Dependencies use patterns instead of CQs.

Definition 4.4   An *XML schema mapping* is a triple $\mathcal{M} = (D_s, D_t, \Sigma_{st})$, where D_s is the source DTD, D_t is the target DTD, and Σ_{st} is a set of st-tgds of the form

$$\pi(\bar{x}, \bar{y}) \rightarrow \exists \bar{z} \, \pi'(\bar{x}, \bar{z})$$

where π and π' are (generalized) patterns.

Given a tree S that conforms to D_s and a tree T that conforms to D_t, we say that T is a *solution* for S under $\mathcal{M}$ if (S, T) satisfy all the st-tgds from Σ_{st}, i.e., for every st-tgd $\pi(\bar{x}, \bar{y}) \rightarrow \exists \bar{z}\, \pi'(\bar{x}, \bar{z})$ in Σ_{st}, whenever $S \models \pi(\bar{a}, \bar{b})$, there exists a tuple of values $\bar{c}$ such that $T \models \pi'(\bar{a}, \bar{c})$. We denote the set of all solutions under $\mathcal{M}$ for S by $\text{Sol}_{\mathcal{M}}(S)$.

The semantics of $\mathcal{M}$ is defined as a binary relation

$$[\![\mathcal{M}]\!] = \{(S, T) \mid S \models D_s,\ T \models D_t,\ T \in \text{Sol}_{\mathcal{M}}(S)\}.$$

□

Example 4.5   Let D_s be the familiar DTD

$$\begin{array}{rclcl}
\text{europe} & \rightarrow & \text{country}^* & \quad \text{country} : @\text{name} \\
\text{country} & \rightarrow & \text{ruler}^* & \quad \text{ruler} : @\text{name}
\end{array}$$

and let D_t be

$$\begin{array}{rclcl}
\text{rulers} & \rightarrow & \text{ruler}^* & \quad \text{ruler} : @\text{name} \\
\text{ruler} & \rightarrow & \text{successor} & \quad \text{successor} : @\text{name}
\end{array}$$

Assuming the rulers are stored in the chronological order on the source side, a natural schema mapping $\mathcal{M}$ might be defined with the following st-tgd:

$$\text{europe}[\text{ruler}(x) \rightarrow \text{ruler}(y)] \longrightarrow \text{rulers}/\text{ruler}(x)/\text{successor}(y).$$

A natural solution for T_1, shown in Fig. 4.1, is the tree T_2 in Fig. 4.3. As we already know, every tree obtained from T_2 by adding new children with arbitrary data values, or by permuting the existing children, is also a solution for T_1. For instance, T_3 in Fig. 4.3 is as good a solution for T_1 as any.   □

The XML mappings we have just defined naturally generalize the usual relational mappings. If we have relational schemas $\mathbf{R_s}$ and $\mathbf{R_t}$, they can be represented as DTDs D_s and D_t: for example, for $\mathbf{R_s} = \{S_1(A, B), S_2(C, D)\}$, the DTD D_s has rules $r \rightarrow s_1, s_2;\ s_1 \rightarrow t_1^*;\ s_2 \rightarrow t_2^*$, as well as $t_1, t_2 \rightarrow \varepsilon$, with t_1 having attributes A, B, and t_2 having attributes C, D. Then each conjunctive query over a schema is easily translated into a pattern over the corresponding DTD together with some equality constraints. For example, $S_1(x, y), S_2(y, z)$ will be translated into

$$r\,[s_1/t_1(x, y_1),\ s_2/t_2(y_2, z)],\ y_1 = y_2.$$

Of course, equalities can be incorporated into the pattern (i.e., by $r[s_1/t_1(x, y),\ s_2/t_2(y, z)])$, but as we said, we often prefer to list them separately to make classification of different types of schema mappings easier. Note also that these patterns use neither the descendant relation nor the horizontal navigation nor inequalities.

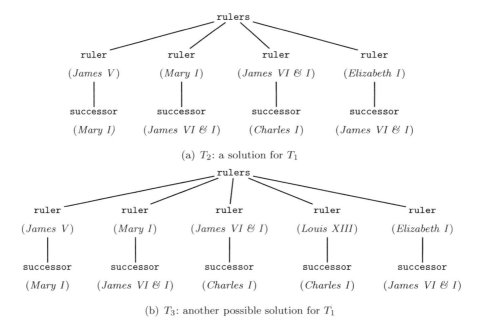

(a) T_2: a solution for T_1

(b) T_3: another possible solution for T_1

Figure 4.3: Solutions for T_1 under $\mathcal{M}$

Classification of schema mappings   We often need to restrict the features available in st-tgds. Using the notation for patterns, we write $\mathrm{SM}(\Pi(\sigma_1), \Pi(\sigma_2))$ to denote the class of mappings where source side patterns come from $\Pi(\sigma_1)$ and target side patterns come from $\Pi(\sigma_2)$. To keep the notation as light as possible, we usually just write $\mathrm{SM}(\sigma_1; \sigma_2)$, and $\mathrm{SM}(\sigma)$ if $\sigma_1 = \sigma_2 = \sigma$.

For reasons to be explained shortly, we work extensively with *nested relational schema mappings*, i.e., schema mappings whose target DTDs are nested relational. By $\mathrm{SM}^{\mathrm{nr}}(\sigma_1; \sigma_2)$, we denote the class of nested relational schema mappings in $\mathrm{SM}(\sigma_1; \sigma_2)$.

If we use the standard XML encoding of relational databases, then relational schema mappings fall into the class $\mathrm{SM}^{\mathrm{nr}}(\downarrow, =)$.

We also write $\mathrm{SM}^\circ(\sigma_1; \sigma_2)$ for mappings where st-tgds in Σ_{st} do not mention attribute values, i.e., where all pattern formulae are of the form $\ell[\lambda]$. These will be useful for establishing hardness results, telling us that structural properties alone make certain problems infeasible.

We now move to the complexity of schema mappings and, just like for patterns, consider two flavors of it.

- *Data complexity of schema mappings* is the data complexity of the *membership problem*: For a fixed mapping $\mathcal{M}$, check, for two trees S, T, whether $(S, T) \in [\![\mathcal{M}]\!]$.

- *Combined complexity of schema mappings* is the combined complexity of the membership problem: Check, for two trees S, T and a mapping $\mathcal{M}$, whether $(S, T) \in \llbracket \mathcal{M} \rrbracket$.

Compared to patterns, the data complexity remains low; the combined complexity jumps to the second level of the polynomial hierarchy, but the parameter that makes it jump there is the number of variables in st-tgds. If we fix that number, even the combined complexity is tractable.

Theorem 4.6   *For XML schema mappings*

- *the data complexity is* LOGSPACE-*complete;*

- *the combined complexity is* Π_2^p-*complete;*

- *the combined complexity is in* PTIME *if the maximum number of variables per pattern is fixed.*

Proof. (1) Checking if a given tree conforms to a DTD amounts to checking if the sequence of children of every node belongs to the language given by the appropriate regular expression. This can be done in LOGSPACE if the DTD is fixed.

Let us now see how to check if S and T satisfy a single constraint $\pi(\bar{x}, \bar{y}) \to \exists \bar{z}\, \pi'(\bar{x}, \bar{z})$. Let $\bar{x} = x_1, x_2, \ldots, x_k$, $\bar{y} = y_1, y_2, \ldots, y_\ell$, and $\bar{z} = z_1, z_2, \ldots, z_m$. Let A be the set of data values used in S or T. We need to check that for each $\bar{a} \in A^k$ and each $\bar{b} \in A^\ell$ such that $S \models \pi[\bar{a}, \bar{b}]$ there exists $\bar{c} \in A^m$ such that $T \models \pi'[\bar{a}, \bar{c}]$. Since the numbers k, ℓ, m are fixed (as parts of the fixed mapping), the space needed for storing all three valuations is logarithmic in the size of S and T. Using Proposition 4.2, we obtain a LOGSPACE algorithm by simply iterating over all possible valuations $\bar{a}$, $\bar{b}$, and $\bar{c}$. LOGSPACE-hardness is shown in the same way as in the proof of Proposition 4.2.

(2) Checking conformance to DTDs can be done in PTIME. Let us concentrate on verifying the dependencies. Consider the following algorithm for the complementary problem: guess a dependency $\pi(\bar{x}, \bar{y}) \to \exists \bar{z}\, \pi'(\bar{x}, \bar{z})$ and tuples $\bar{a}, \bar{b}$, and check that $S \models \pi(\bar{a}, \bar{b})$ and $T \not\models \exists \bar{z}\, \pi'(\bar{a}, \bar{z})$. By Proposition 4.2, the first check is polynomial. The second check, however, involves a tree pattern possibly containing variables, so it can only be done in coNP. Altogether, the algorithm is in Π_2^p. Hardness can be obtained via a reduction from the validity of Π_2 quantified boolean formulae.

(3) Proceed just like in (1). The numbers of variables per pattern is bounded, so there are only polynomially many possible valuations. Hence, we may iterate over all of them using algorithm from Proposition 4.2 to check $S \models \pi[\bar{a}, \bar{b}]$ and $T \models \pi'[\bar{a}, \bar{c}]$. $\square$

4.3   STATIC ANALYSIS OF XML SCHEMA MAPPINGS

4.3.1   CONSISTENCY

As we already mentioned, XML schema mappings may be inconsistent: there are mappings $\mathcal{M}$ so that $\llbracket \mathcal{M} \rrbracket = \emptyset$, i.e., no tree has a solution. In addition to consistent mappings, in which *some* trees have solutions, we would like to consider mappings in which *every* tree has a solution. These are very desirable for a variety of reasons: not only are we guaranteed to have possible target documents for every possible source, but the property is also preserved when we compose mappings.

We start by analyzing consistency. We say that a mapping is *consistent* if $[\![\mathcal{M}]\!] \neq \emptyset$; that is, if $\text{Sol}_{\mathcal{M}}(S) \neq \emptyset$ for some $S \models D_s$. The main problem we consider is the following:

PROBLEM: $\text{Cons}(\sigma)$
INPUT: A mapping $\mathcal{M} = (D_s, D_t, \Sigma_{st}) \in \text{SM}(\sigma)$
QUESTION: Is $\mathcal{M}$ consistent?

If we use $\text{SM}^\circ(\sigma)$ instead of $\text{SM}(\sigma)$ (i.e., if we use mappings in which attribute values are not mentioned at all), we denote the consistency problem by $\text{Cons}^\circ(\sigma)$.

In the consistency analysis, several tools from automata theory are useful. We recall them now briefly. We assume that the reader is familiar with the notion of finite automata on words. We write NFA and DFA for non-deterministic and deterministic finite automata. If $\mathcal{A}$ is an automaton, then $L(\mathcal{A})$ is the language accepted by it. Recall that, given a regular expression e, constructing an NFA $\mathcal{A}_e$ with $L(\mathcal{A}_e) = L(e)$ can be done in polynomial time. Finding an equivalent DFA can be done in exponential time via the well known powerset construction.

A nondeterministic (ranked) finite tree automaton (NFTA) on binary node-labeled trees over alphabet Γ is defined as $\mathcal{A} = \langle Q, q_0, \delta, F \rangle$ where Q is the set of states, $q_0 \in Q$, $F \subseteq Q$ and $\delta : \Gamma \times Q \times Q \to 2^Q$ is the transition function. Given a binary tree T, a run of $\mathcal{A}$ on T is a function $\rho_{\mathcal{A}} : T \to Q$ that assigns states to nodes. For a leaf s labeled a, we require that $\rho_{\mathcal{A}}(s) \in \delta(a, q_0, q_0)$, and for a node s labeled a with two children s_1 and s_2, we require that $\rho_{\mathcal{A}}(s) \in \delta(a, \rho_{\mathcal{A}}(s_1), \rho_{\mathcal{A}}(s_2))$. A tree T is accepted if there is a run $\rho_{\mathcal{A}}$ such that $\rho_{\mathcal{A}}(\text{root}) \in F$. Given an NFTA $\mathcal{A}$, testing whether $L(\mathcal{A}) = \emptyset$ can be done in time linear in the size of $\mathcal{A}$. *Nonuniversality* of $\mathcal{A}$ (testing whether there is a tree not accepted by $\mathcal{A}$) is Exptime-complete.

An unranked nondeterministic finite tree automaton (UNFTA) on ordered unranked node-labeled trees over alphabet Γ is defined as $\mathcal{A} = \langle Q, \delta, F \rangle$ where Q is the set of states, $F \subseteq Q$ and $\delta : Q \times \Gamma \to 2^{Q^*}$ is the transition function such that $\delta(q, a)$ is a regular language for every $s \in Q$ and $a \in \Gamma$. Given an ordered unranked tree T, a run of $\mathcal{A}$ on T is again a function $\rho_{\mathcal{A}} : T \to Q$ that assigns states to nodes. If s is a node whose children are $s_1, \ldots, s_n$ ordered by the sibling relation as $s_1 \to \ldots \to s_n$, then the word $\rho_{\mathcal{A}}(s_1) \ldots \rho_{\mathcal{A}}(s_n)$ over Q must be in $\delta(\rho_{\mathcal{A}}(s), a)$. In particular, if s is a leaf, then a run can assign a state q to it iff $\varepsilon \in L(\delta(q, a))$. A tree T is accepted if there is a run $\rho_{\mathcal{A}}$ such that $\rho_{\mathcal{A}}(\text{root}) \in F$. An automaton is deterministic if every tree admits only one run.

The standard representation of UNFTAs uses NFAs for transitions, that is, δ maps pairs state-letter to NFAs over Q. It is known that testing nonemptiness is again polynomial-time [Neven, 2002]. If an automaton is deterministic and furthermore all transitions are represented by DFAs, then we refer to UFTA(DFA).

DTDs can naturally be represented by tree automata. We shall consider DTDs without attributes. Such a DTD D over a set E of element types is represented by an automaton $\mathcal{A}_D$, in which the set of states is E, and $\delta(\ell, \ell)$ is defined to be an automaton for $P(\ell)$, and $\delta(\ell, \ell') = \emptyset$, otherwise, and $F = \{r\}$. In exponential time, one can determinize the automata representing regular expressions in productions and obtain an equivalent UFTA(DFA).

As tree automata do not look at data values at all, we cannot hope to do the same for general tree patterns; we need to assume the patterns do not talk about data values either.

Lemma 4.7   *For every pattern π without variables, one can compute in exponential time a UFTA(DFA) $\mathcal{A}_\pi$ such that $L(\mathcal{A}_\pi) = \{T \mid T \models \pi\}$.*

Proof. We construct $\mathcal{A}_\pi$ by induction on the structure of π. If $\pi = \ell$ with $\ell \in \Gamma \cup \{\_\}$, the claim follows easily. Assume we have an automaton $\mathcal{A}_\pi = \langle Q, \delta, F \rangle$ for π. To obtain $\mathcal{A}_{//\pi}$ add a fresh state f, set $\delta^{//\pi}(f, a) = Q^*(F \cup \{f\})Q^*$ for every $a \in \Gamma$ (the equivalent DFA has two states), $\delta^{//\pi}(q, a) = \delta(q, a) \cap (Q - F)^*$ for every $a \in \Gamma$, $q \in Q$ (equivalent DFAs grow by at most one state), and $F^{//\pi} = F \cup \{f\}$.

The last case is that of $\pi = \ell[\mu_1, \dots, \mu_n]$. Let us first construct an automaton for $\ell[\mu]$ with

$$\mu = (\pi_1 \to \cdots \to \pi_{k_1}) \to^* (\pi_{k_1+1} \to \cdots \to \pi_{k_2}) \to^* \cdots \to^* (\pi_{k_{m-1}+1} \to \cdots \to \pi_{k_m}).$$

Assume that we have already constructed $\mathcal{A}_{\pi_j} = \langle Q_j, \delta_j, F_j \rangle$ for each π_j. The state space of $\mathcal{A}_{\ell[\mu]}$ is $Q = Q_1 \times Q_2 \times \cdots \times Q_{k_m} \times \{\top, \bot\}$. Consider the language M defined by the regular expression

$$Q^*(\tilde{F}_1 \tilde{F}_2 \cdots \tilde{F}_{k_1})Q^*(\tilde{F}_{k_1+1} \tilde{F}_{k_1+2} \cdots \tilde{F}_{k_2})Q^* \cdots Q^*(\tilde{F}_{k_{m-1}+1} \tilde{F}_{k_{m-1}+2} \cdots \tilde{F}_{k_m})Q^*,$$

where $\tilde{F}_j = \{(q_1, \dots, q_{k_m+1}) \in Q \mid q_j \in F_j\}$. It is not difficult to construct a NFA with $\mathcal{O}(k_m)$ states recognizing M; standard determinization gives an equivalent DFA $\mathcal{B}$ with $2^{\mathcal{O}(k_m)}$ states. $\mathcal{A}_{\ell[\mu]}$'s transition relation is now defined as

$$\delta((\bar{q}, s), a) = (\delta_1(q_1, a) \times \delta_2(q_2, a) \times \cdots \times \delta_{k_m}(q_{k_m}, a) \times \{\top, \bot\}) \cap K$$

where $K = M$ if $s = \top$, $a = \ell$ (or $\ell = \_$), and $K = Q^* - M$, otherwise. Each such transition can be represented by a product of automata $\mathcal{B}_1, \dots, \mathcal{B}_n$ and $\mathcal{B}$ (or its complement), where B_j are single exponential in $\|\pi_j\|$, and $\mathcal{B}$ is single exponential in k_m. Since $\|\pi\|$ is roughly $\sum_{j=1}^n \|\pi_j\|$, the size of the product automaton $\prod_{j=1}^m \|\mathcal{B}_j\| \cdot \|\mathcal{B}\|$ is single exponential in $\|\pi\|$. The accepting states are those with $\top$ as the last component. In order to obtain an automaton for $\ell[\mu_1, \mu_2, \dots, \mu_n]$, it suffices to take the product of $\mathcal{A}_{\ell[\mu_i]}$.

Verifying that the construction is single exponential is left to the reader.   □

The tools we have developed can be applied directly to the consistency problem.

Proposition 4.8   Cons°($\downarrow, \downarrow^*, \to, \to^*, \_$) *is* Exptime-*complete.*

Proof. For a mapping (D_s, D_t, Σ_{st}) to be consistent, there must exist a pair (T_1, T_2) such that for all $\varphi \to \psi \in \Sigma_{st}$ it holds that $T_1 \models \varphi$ implies $T_2 \models \psi$. Suppose $\Sigma_{st} = \{\varphi_i \to \psi_i \mid i = 1, 2, \dots, n\}$. Then the existence of such a pair is equivalent to the existence of a subset $I \subseteq \{1, 2, \dots, n\}$ satisfying

- there exists $T_1 \models D_s$ such that $T_1 \not\models \varphi_j$ for all $j \notin I$,

- there exists $T_2 \models D_t$ such that $T_2 \models \psi_i$ for all $i \in I$.

This amounts to nonemptiness of the following automata:

- $A_{D_s} \times \prod_{j \notin I} \bar{A}_{\varphi_j}$,

- $A_{D_t} \times \prod_{j \in I} A_{\psi_j}$.

The construction of each A_φ takes exponential time. Since A_φ are deterministic, complementing them is straightforward. Testing nonemptiness of $A_1 \times \cdots \times A_k$ can be done in time $\mathcal{O}(|A_1| \times \cdots \times |A_k|)$. Hence, the overall complexity is EXPTIME.

To prove EXPTIME-hardness, we provide a reduction from the nonuniversality problem for tree automata. The idea of the encoding is that the source tree codes both an input tree and the run of the corresponding deterministic powerset automaton. The st-tgds ensure that the run is constructed properly, and that it contains only non-final states in the root.

Let $\Gamma = \{a_1, \ldots, a_k\}$ be the alphabet, and let $\mathcal{A} = (Q, q_0, \delta, F)$ where $Q = \{q_0, \ldots, q_n\}$. The source DTD D_s is

$$
\begin{aligned}
\texttt{r}, \texttt{left}, \texttt{right} \quad &\rightarrow \quad \texttt{label}\, q_0 \ldots q_n\,(\texttt{left}\,\texttt{right}\mid\texttt{leaf}) \\
\texttt{label} \quad &\rightarrow \quad a_1 \mid a_2 \mid \ldots \mid a_k \\
q_1, q_2, \ldots, q_n \quad &\rightarrow \quad \texttt{yes}\mid\texttt{no}
\end{aligned}
$$

and the target DTD D_t is simply $\texttt{r} \rightarrow \varepsilon$.

In every tree conforming to D_s, the nodes labeled with $\texttt{r}$, $\texttt{left}$ and $\texttt{right}$ form a binary tree over which we run the powerset automaton. A q_i-child should lead to a $\texttt{yes}$ iff the state of the powerset automaton contains q_i. This is ensured by the st-tgds

$$
//\_[q_k/\texttt{no},\ \texttt{label}/a_l,\ \texttt{left}/q_i/\texttt{yes},\ \texttt{right}/q_j/\texttt{yes}] \rightarrow \perp \qquad \text{for } q_k \in \delta(a_l, q_i, q_j)
$$

where $\perp$ is a fixed pattern inconsistent with D_t, e.g., $\texttt{r}/\texttt{r}$. Similarly, we enforce that every state, in which $\mathcal{A}$ can be after reading a leaf with a given label, is a $\texttt{yes}$-state:

$$
//\_[q_k/\texttt{no},\ \texttt{label}/a_l,\ \texttt{leaf}] \rightarrow \perp \qquad \text{for } q_k \in \delta(a_l, q_0, q_0).
$$

Finally, we check that in the root of the run only non-finite states are present:

$$
\texttt{r}/q_k/\texttt{yes} \rightarrow \perp \qquad \text{for } q_k \in Q - F.
$$

The obtained mapping is consistent iff there is a tree not accepted by $\mathcal{A}$. $\square$

Using a very simple observation, we can immediately extend the algorithm presented above to the case with variables, provided that data comparisons are not allowed.

Theorem 4.9 *The problem* CONS$(\downarrow, \downarrow^*, \rightarrow, \rightarrow^*, \_)$ *is solvable in* EXPTIME *(and thus it is* EXPTIME-*complete).*

Proof. In the absence of data comparisons, we can simply "forget" about the data values. For a tree pattern π, let π° denote a tree pattern obtained from π by replacing all subformulae of the form $\ell(\bar{t})$ with ℓ, for ℓ being a label or _ . Let $\Sigma_{st}^\circ = \{\pi_1^\circ \to \pi_2^\circ \mid (\pi_1 \to \exists \bar{z}\, \pi_2) \in \Sigma_{st}\}$. It is not difficult to see that (D_S, D_T, Σ_{st}) is consistent if and only if $(D_S, D_T, \Sigma_{st}^\circ)$ is consistent.   □

The high complexity of consistency is discouraging, but it turns out that we can ensure tractability by allowing only nested-relational DTDs. Unfortunately, this works for downward navigation only, once we add even the simplest form of horizontal navigation ($\to$), we lose tractability. We leave the proof of the following proposition as an exercise.

Proposition 4.10   *Under restriction to nested-relational DTDs*

- $\textsc{Cons}(\downarrow, \downarrow^*, \_)$ *is solvable in polynomial (cubic) time;*

- $\textsc{Cons}(\downarrow, \downarrow^*, \to)$ *is* Pspace-*hard.*

We now move to classes of schema mappings that allow comparisons of attribute values. It is common to lose decidability (or low complexity solutions) of static analysis problems once data values and their comparisons are considered. Here we witness a similar situation: having either descendant or next-sibling, together with either $=$ or $\neq$, leads to undecidability of consistency.

Theorem 4.11   *Each of the following problems is undecidable:* $\textsc{Cons}(\downarrow, \downarrow^*, =)$, $\textsc{Cons}(\downarrow, \downarrow^*, \neq)$, $\textsc{Cons}(\downarrow, \to, =)$, *and* $\textsc{Cons}(\downarrow, \to, \neq)$.

Proof. We only prove undecidability of $\textsc{Cons}(\downarrow, \downarrow^*, =)$. The remaining cases are left as an exercise. We describe a reduction from halting problem of 2-register machine, which is known to be undecidable. That is, given a 2-register machine (defined below), we construct a schema mapping that is consistent iff the machine halts. Trees encoding runs of a 2-register machine will be of the form:

$$
\begin{array}{ccc}
 & r & \\
\diagup & & \diagdown \\
I_1(0,0) & & R(0) \\
\mid & & \mid \\
I_1(1,0) & & R(1) \\
\vdots & & \vdots
\end{array}
$$

Intuitively, the left branch is meant to represent sequence of states with data values representing registers while the right one is a sequence to represent natural numbers. We do not have any equality test against a constant (say, a natural number). So, what we really do is simulate values by the depth from the root. More concretely, 0 and 1 above might as well be $\sharp$ and $\flat$. Whatever they are, we simply take the value at the 0th level as 0 and the 1st level as 1, and so on. The above tree can be easily described by a DTD. To make sure it is a proper run of the given machine, we use st-tgds to check that the registers change their values according to legal transitions.

Let us now describe the reduction in detail. A 2-register machine M consists of a set of states $Q = \{1, 2, \ldots, f\}$, a list of instructions $\mathcal{I} = \langle I_i \mid i \in Q \setminus \{f\}\rangle$ (one instruction for each state apart from the last state f), and two registers r_1 and r_2, each containing a natural number. An instantaneous description (ID) of M is a triple $\langle i, m, n \rangle$ where $i \in Q$ and $m, n \in \mathbb{N}$ are natural numbers stored in r_1 and r_2, respectively.

An instruction of 2-register machine is either *increment* or *decrement*, and defines the transition relation $\rightarrow_M$ between IDs.

increment $I_i = \langle r, j \rangle$, where $i \in Q$ and r is one of r_1 and r_2. This means that M in state i increments r and goes to state j:

$$\langle i, m, n \rangle \rightarrow_M \begin{cases} \langle j, m + 1, n \rangle & \text{if } r = r_1, \\ \langle j, m, n + 1 \rangle & \text{if } r = r_2. \end{cases}$$

decrement $I_i = \langle r, j, k \rangle$, where $i, j, k \in Q$ and r is one of the two registers. This means that M in state i can test whether r is 0, and go to state j if it is, or decrement r and go to k if it is not. In symbols,

$$\langle i, m, n \rangle \rightarrow_M \begin{cases} \langle j, 0, n \rangle & \text{if } r = r_1 \text{ and } m = 0, \\ \langle j, m - 1, n \rangle & \text{if } r = r_1 \text{ and } m \neq 0, \\ \langle j, m, 0 \rangle & \text{if } r = r_2 \text{ and } n = 0, \\ \langle j, m, n - 1 \rangle & \text{if } r = r_2 \text{ and } n \neq 0. \end{cases}$$

The initial ID is $\langle 1, 0, 0 \rangle$ and the final ID is $\langle f, 0, 0 \rangle$. The halting problem for 2-register machine is to decide, given a 2-register machine M, whether $\langle 1, 0, 0 \rangle \rightarrow_M^* \langle f, 0, 0 \rangle$.

Let us now describe how to construct a mapping, which is consistent iff the given machine halts. The source DTD D_s over the alphabet $\{r, I_1, I_2, \ldots, I_f, R, \sharp\}$ is given by

$$\begin{aligned} r &\rightarrow I_1 R \\ I_i &\rightarrow I_j & \text{for all } i \text{ such that } I_i = \langle r, j \rangle \\ I_i &\rightarrow I_j | I_k & \text{for all } i \text{ such that } I_i = \langle r, j, k \rangle \\ R &\rightarrow R | \sharp \\ I_f, \sharp &\rightarrow \varepsilon \end{aligned}$$

where each I_i has two attributes corresponding to the values of the registers, and R has one attribute. The target DTD D_t is simply $\{r \rightarrow \varepsilon\}$. The st-tgds Σ_{st} are described below.

As mentioned above, the sequence of R's is meant to be that of natural numbers, but what represents a number is the depth in the tree instead of a value itself. In other words, the data values are used as indices, so they must be unique. The following disallows two values to appear more than once.

$$// R(x) // R(x) \rightarrow \bot$$

Let us now deal with the left branch, which is meant to encode the run itself. We have assumed that the initial ID is $\langle 1, 0, 0 \rangle$; the constraints below exclude other situations.

$$r[I_1(x, y), //R/R(x)] \rightarrow \bot$$
$$r[I_1(x, y), //R/R(y)] \rightarrow \bot$$

Now, let us check that we proceed correctly. For each i such that $I_i = \langle r_1, j \rangle$, we need to enforce that there is a number in the R-branch to set the value of r_1 to, and that the next configuration is indeed obtained by increasing r_1.

$$r[//I_i(x, y), //R(x)/\sharp] \rightarrow \bot$$
$$r[//I_i(x, y)/I_j(x', y'), //R(x)/R(x'')] \rightarrow x' = x'', \ y' = y$$

For each i such that $I_i = \langle r_1, j, k \rangle$, we need to say: if the next state is k, then r_1 stores 0, and both registers stay the same; if the next state is j, then r_1 does not store 0, the register r_1 gets decreased, and r_2 stays the same.

$$r[//I_i(x, y)/I_k(x', y'), R(x'')] \rightarrow x = x'', \ x' = x, \ y' = y$$
$$r[//I_i(x, y)/I_j, R(x)] \rightarrow \bot$$
$$r[//I_i(x, y)/I_j(x', y'), //R(x'')/R(x)] \rightarrow x' = x'', \ y' = y$$

For each i such that $I_i = \langle r_2, j \rangle$ or $I_i = \langle r_2, j, k \rangle$ we add analogous st-tgds.

Finally, we have to make sure that we end properly. In each source tree, the left branch must end with I_f, so we do not need to check that. It is enough to say that both registers are set to 0.

$$r[//I_i(x, y)/\sharp, //R/R(x)] \rightarrow \bot$$
$$r[//I_i(x, y)/\sharp, //R/R(y)] \rightarrow \bot$$

The obtained mapping (D_s, D_t, Σ_{st}) is consistent iff there is a halting run of the given 2-register machine. Thus we have proved that $\text{CONS}(\downarrow^*, =)$ is undecidable. □

This result raises the question whether there is any useful decidable restriction of the consistency problem. Again, nested-relational DTDs give us a decidable restriction, but only for downward navigation.

Theorem 4.12 *Under the restriction to nested-relational DTDs:*

- *the problem* $\text{CONS}(\downarrow, \downarrow^*, =, \neq, \_)$ *is* NEXPTIME-*complete;*
- *the problem* $\text{CONS}(\downarrow, \rightarrow, =)$ *is undecidable.*

The lower bound for $\text{CONS}(\downarrow, \downarrow^*, =, \neq, \_)$ is obtained via a reduction from Bernays-Schönfinkel satisfiability problem, i.e., satisfiability of first order formulae of the form

$$\exists x_1 \cdots \exists x_m \forall x_{m+1} \cdots \forall x_n \bigwedge_{i=1}^{k} \bigvee_{j=1}^{\ell} C_{i,j},$$

where C_{ij} is an atom or a negated atom. The upper bound is obtained by providing single exponential trees (S, T) witnessing consistency. A modification of the 2-register machine reduction gives the undecidability result.

	arbitrary DTDs	nested relational DTDs
CONS $(\Downarrow, \_)$	EXPTIME-complete	PTIME
CONS $(\Downarrow, \Rightarrow, \_)$	EXPTIME-complete	PSPACE-hard (even for CONS $(\Downarrow, \rightarrow)$)
CONS $(\Downarrow, =, \_)$	undecidable	NEXPTIME-complete (even with $\neq$)
CONS $(\Downarrow, \Rightarrow, =, \_)$	undecidable	undecidable
ABCONS $(\Downarrow, \_)$	in EXPSPACE; NEXPTIME-hard	PTIME for ABCONS $(\downarrow)$

Figure 4.4: Complexity of consistency problems

4.3.2   ABSOLUTE CONSISTENCY

We now switch to a stronger notion of consistency. Recall that a mapping is consistent if some tree S that conforms to the source DTD D_s has a solution. We say that $\mathcal{M}$ is *absolutely consistent* if *every* tree T that conforms to the source DTD D_s has a solution. That is, $\text{SOL}_{\mathcal{M}}(S) \neq \emptyset$ for all $S \models D_s$. We consider the problem:

PROBLEM:	ABCONS(σ)
INPUT:	Mapping $\mathcal{M} = (D_s, D_t, \Sigma_{st}) \in \text{SM}(\sigma)$
QUESTION:	Is $\mathcal{M}$ absolutely consistent?

Reasoning about the complexity of absolute consistency is significantly harder than reasoning about the consistency problem. We know that CONS$(\Downarrow)$ can be easily reduced to CONS$^{\circ}(\Downarrow)$. However, eliminating data values does not work for absolute consistency. Indeed, consider a mapping with the source DTD $r \rightarrow a^*$, $a \rightarrow \varepsilon$ and the target DTD $r \rightarrow a$, $a \rightarrow \varepsilon$, with a having a single attribute. Let the st-tgd be $r/a(x) \rightarrow r/a(x)$. This mapping $\mathcal{M}$ is not absolutely consistent: take, for example, a source tree with two different values of the attribute. But stripping $\mathcal{M}$ of data values, i.e., replacing the st-tgd by $r/a \rightarrow r/a$, makes it absolutely consistent.

Thus, we cannot use purely automata-theoretic techniques for reasoning about absolute consistency, even for downward navigation. In fact, the above example indicates that to reason about absolute consistency even in that case, we need to reason about counts of occurrences of different data values.

Nevertheless, let us first look at the case $\mathrm{AbCons}^\circ(\Downarrow)$, i.e., checking absolute consistency of mappings $\mathcal{M}^\circ$ in which all references to attribute values have been removed. Slightly surprisingly, it has lower complexity than $\mathrm{Cons}^\circ(\Downarrow)$.

Proposition 4.13 $\mathrm{AbCons}^\circ(\Downarrow)$ *is* Π_2^p-*complete.*

Proof. The set of dependencies Σ_{st} is of the form $\{\pi_i \to \pi_i'\}_{i \in I}$, where patterns have no variables. To check consistency of such a mapping, we need to check whether there exists a set $J \subseteq I$ so that D_t and all the π_j', $j \in J$ are satisfiable, while D_s together with the *negations* of π_k, $k \notin J$, are satisfiable. This makes consistency ExpTime-complete (see Proposition 4.8). For absolute consistency, we only need to verify that there does not exist $J \subseteq I$ so that D_s and π_j, $j \in J$, are satisfiable but D_t and π_j', $j \in J$, are not. Notice that absolute consistency eliminates the need for checking satisfiability of negations of patterns. Since satisfiability of patterns and DTDs is in NP, the above shows that absolute consistency of mappings $\mathcal{M}^\circ$ is in Π_2^p. Proving hardness is an instructive exercise.   □

As suggested by the example, the problem becomes much harder if we allow variables:

Theorem 4.14 $\mathrm{AbCons}(\Downarrow)$ *is decidable. In fact, the problem is in* ExpSpace *and* NexpTime-*hard.*

The proof of this result is based on rather involved analysis of a data structure that counts possible numbers of occurrences of attribute values. The lower bound does not match the upper bound, but it does tell us that any algorithm for solving $\mathrm{AbCons}(\Downarrow)$ will run in double-exponential time, and hence will be impractical unless restrictions are imposed.

Restrictions to nested-relational DTDs often worked for us, but in this case, they alone do not suffice: we shall also need to forbid _ and $\downarrow^*$. If we relax any of the restrictions, the complexity goes back to NexpTime-hardness:

Theorem 4.15   *Over nested relational DTDs the problem* $\mathrm{AbCons}(\downarrow)$ *is solvable in* PTime. *If the mappings are allowed to use either the wildcard or the descendant, the problem becomes* NexpTime-*hard.*

An abridged summary of the complexity results related to the consistency problem is given in Fig. 4.4.

4.4   EXCHANGE WITH XML SCHEMA MAPPINGS

4.4.1   DATA EXCHANGE PROBLEM

The ultimate goal of data exchange is to answer queries over target data in a way consistent with the source data. Just like in the relational case, we study conjunctive queries and their unions. As we have learned, it is convenient to work with tree patterns, which have very similar expressivity. Thus, for querying XML documents we use the same language as for the dependencies: tree patterns with equalities and inequalities, to capture the analog of relational conjunctive queries (with inequalities). And, of course, we allow projection.

That is, a query Q is an expression of the form

$$\exists \bar{y} \; \pi(\bar{x}, \bar{y}),$$

where π is a (generalized) tree pattern. The semantics is defined in the standard way. The output of the query is the set of those valuations of free variables that make the query hold true

$$Q(T) = \left\{ \bar{a} \mid T \models \exists \bar{y} \, \pi(\bar{a}, \bar{y}) \right\} .$$

This class of queries is denoted by **CTQ** (conjunctive tree queries). Note that **CTQ** is indeed closed under conjunctions, due to the semantics of λ, λ' in patterns.

We also consider unions of such queries: **UCTQ** denotes the class of queries of the form $Q_1(\bar{x}) \cup \cdots \cup Q_m(\bar{x})$, where each Q_i is a query from **CTQ**. Like for schema mappings, we write **CTQ** (σ) and **UCTQ** (σ) for $\sigma \subseteq \{\downarrow, \downarrow^*, \rightarrow, \rightarrow^*, =, \neq, \_\}$ to denote the subclass of queries using only the symbols from σ. Recall that we are using abbreviations $\Downarrow$ for $(\downarrow, \downarrow^*)$ and $\Rightarrow$ for $(\rightarrow, \rightarrow^*)$.

Example 4.16   Recall the mapping defined in Example 4.5. Suppose we want to find out which rulers succeeded more than one other ruler. This can be expressed over the target schema by the following conjunctive query MultiSucc:

$$\exists x \; \exists y \; \texttt{rulers}[\texttt{ruler}(x)/\texttt{successor}(z), \texttt{ruler}(y)/\texttt{successor}(z)] \wedge x \neq y .$$

Just like in the relational case, the query might return different answers on different solutions to a given source tree. For instance, for the source tree T_1 shown in Fig. 4.1, two possible solutions are T_2 and T_3 shown in Fig. 4.3. On T_2 the query MultiSucc returns {*James VI & I*}, and on T_3 the answer is {*James VI & I*, *Charles I*}. □

What is the right answer to a query then? Since the queries return tuples of values, we can simply adapt the *certain answers semantics* from the relational case. For a mapping $\mathcal{M}$, a query Q, and a source tree S conforming to D_s, we return the tuples which would be returned for every possible solution:

$$certain_{\mathcal{M}}(Q, S) = \bigcap \left\{ Q(T) \mid T \text{ is a solution for } S \text{ under } \mathcal{M} \right\} .$$

The subscript $\mathcal{M}$ is omitted when it is clear from the context.

In our running example,

$$certain_{\mathcal{M}}(\texttt{MultiSucc}, T_1) = \{\textit{James VI \& I}\} .$$

Note that when Q is a Boolean query, $certain_{\mathcal{M}}(Q, S)$ is true if and only if Q is true for all the solutions.

We are interested in the following decision problem, for fixed $\mathcal{M}$ and Q:

PROBLEM:	CERTAIN$_{\mathcal{M}}(Q)$
INPUT:	a source tree S, a tuple $\bar{s}$
QUESTION:	$\bar{s} \in certain_{\mathcal{M}}(Q, S)$?

We have seen that in the relational case certain answers problem for CQs with inequalities is in coNP. In the XML setting, it is also the case, but the proof is more involved. Below, we only give a sketch of the main ideas.

Proposition 4.17   *For every schema mapping $\mathcal{M}$ from* SM$(\Downarrow, \Rightarrow, =, \neq)$ *and every query Q from* **UCTQ** $(\Downarrow, \Rightarrow, =, \neq)$*, the problem* CERTAIN$_{\mathcal{M}}(Q)$ *is in* coNP.

Proof idea. Take a query $Q \in$ **UCTQ**$^{\neq}$, an XML schema mapping $\mathcal{M} = (D_s, D_t, \Sigma_{st})$, and a source tree S conforming to D_s. Without loss of generality, we can assume that Q is Boolean.

Let A be the set of data values used in S. We can assume that the tuple $\bar{s}$ only uses data values from A (otherwise, the query is trivially false). A tree conforming to the target DTD is a solution for S iff it satisfies every sentence from the following set:

$$\Phi = \{ \exists \bar{z} \, \pi_2(\bar{a}, \bar{z}) \mid (\pi_1(\bar{x}, \bar{y}) \rightarrow \exists \bar{z} \, \pi_2(\bar{x}, \bar{z})) \in \Sigma_{st}, \ \bar{a} \in A^{|\bar{x}|}, \bar{b} \in A^{|\bar{y}|}, \ S \models \pi_1(\bar{a}, \bar{b}) \} \, .$$

(Note that for a fixed mapping the set Φ can be computed in PTIME.) The certain answer to Q is false iff there exists a tree T such that $T \models D_t$, $T \models \Phi$, $T \not\models Q$. Assume that there exists such a counter-example T. Fix a set of nodes witnessing Φ. We will show that we can trim most of the non-witnessing nodes without satisfying Q, or violating D_t, so that T becomes polynomial.

Consider a first order logic formula equivalent to Q, and let k be its quantifier rank. The k-type of a node is the set of all FO formulae it satisfies. It is known that there are only finitely many nonequivalent FO formulae of any given quantifier rank. In consequence, there are only finitely many different k-types. Since k depends only on the query, we have a fixed number of k-types.

Now, roughly, for any pair u, v of non-witnessing nodes with the same FO k-type, we cut the nodes in-between and merge u, v (provided that cutting neither removes any witnessing node nor leads to violation of the DTD). Cutting this way, vertically and horizontally, we make sure all the witnesses are not too far apart, and the resulting tree has polynomial size.   □

The certain answers problem easily becomes coNP-hard. In the next two subsections, we chart its tractability frontier: we investigate the reasons for hardness and isolate a fairly expressive and natural tractable case.

4.4.2   HARDNESS OF QUERY ANSWERING

In this section, we investigate coNP-hard cases of certain answers problem. The reasons for hardness may come from three main sources: DTDs, st-tgds, and queries.

Let us first consider DTDs. It can be shown that for SM$(\downarrow, =)$ and **CTQ** $(\downarrow, =)$, there is a dichotomy in the first parameter: if DTDs allow enough disjunction, the problem is coNP-hard, otherwise, it is polynomial. Without giving the precise characterization of the class of mappings that gives hardness, we show how simple these mappings can be.

We will give examples of an XML schema mapping $\mathcal{M}$ and a Boolean query Q such that 3SAT is reducible to the complement of $\text{CERTAIN}_{\mathcal{M}}(Q)$, i.e., for each 3SAT instance φ

$$certain_{\mathcal{M}}(Q, S_\varphi) \text{ is } \texttt{false} \text{ iff } \varphi \text{ is satisfiable,}$$

where S_φ is a tree encoding of φ described below.

Suppose we are given a 3-CNF formula $\varphi = \bigwedge_{i=1}^{n} \bigvee_{j=1}^{3} c_{ij}$, where c_{ij} is a literal. The tree encoding, S_φ, is best explained on a concrete example. A formula $(x_1 \vee \neg x_3 \vee x_4) \wedge (x_2 \vee x_3 \vee \neg x_4)$ is encoded as

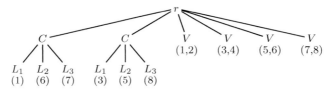

Each V node has two attribute values encoding a variable and its negation with two different values. For example, $V(1, 2)$ indicates that x_1 is encoded by the data value '1' and $\neg x_1$ by '2'. Also for each clause in the formula, we have a C node that has three children labeled L_1, L_2, L_3. L_i holds the data value encoding the ith literal in the clause. In the example above, the second literal of the first clause is $\neg x_3$, and hence the data value of L_1 under the middle C node is '6'.

Let us first see that disjunction in DTDs leads to intractability. In accordance with the encoding above, let D_s be

$$
\begin{aligned}
r &\to C^* V^* & \quad & V : @a_1, @a_2 \\
C &\to L_1 L_2 L_3 & \quad & L_i : @b
\end{aligned}
$$

where $i = 1, 2, 3$. The target DTD D_t is defined as

$$
\begin{aligned}
r &\to C^* V^* & \quad & V : @a_1, @a_2 \\
C &\to L_1 L_2 L_3 & \quad & L_i : @b \\
L_i &\to K \mid N
\end{aligned}
$$

where $i = 1, 2, 3$. The st-tgds Σ_{st} simply copy the tree S_φ in the target, guessing a K-node or an N-node under each L_i-node:

$$
\begin{aligned}
r/C[L_1(x), L_2(y), L_3(z)] &\to r/C[L_1(x), L_2(y), L_3(z)], \\
r/V(x, y) &\to r/V(x, y).
\end{aligned}
$$

K means that the literal is set to $\texttt{true}$, N means it is set to $\texttt{false}$. Now we need to check that either a variable and its negation is set to $\texttt{true}$, or there is a clause with all literals set to $\texttt{false}$. This is done by the following query:

$$\bigcup_{i,j} \exists x \exists y \, r\left[V(x, y), C/L_i(x)/K, C/L_j(y)/K\right] \cup r/C[L_1/N, L_2/N, L_3/N]$$

Next, we show that setting a fixed number of children (greater than 1) with the same label can lead to intractability. This time, the mapping itself is defined so that a solution for S_φ corresponds to a selection of (at least) one literal for each clause in φ. The query only asks if the selection contains a variable and its negation. Thus the existence of a solution falsifying the query implies the existence of a well-defined (partial) assignment that satisfies the formula φ.

The source DTD D_s is as before, and target DTD D_t is:

$$
\begin{aligned}
r &\to C^* V^* & V &: @a_1, @a_2 \\
C &\to LLL & L &: @b \\
L &\to K?
\end{aligned}
$$

The st-tgds Σ_{st} are:

$$
\begin{aligned}
r/C[L_1(x), L_2(y), L_3(z)] &\to r/C[L(x), L(y), L(z), L/K], \\
r/V(x, y) &\to r/V(x, y).
\end{aligned}
$$

Essentially, we copy S_φ in the target, and with a K-child we indicate the chosen literals. As we demand that in each clause at least one literal is chosen, a solution gives a valuation satisfying the formula, provided that we have chosen consistently. This is verified by the query, which is defined as

$$\exists x \exists y \, r\left[V(x, y), C/L(x)/K, C/L(y)/K\right].$$

Clearly, the query is true if a variable and its negation are chosen.

The examples above involve a lot of guessing on where patterns could be put in a target tree. If the mapping is specific enough, this is not possible. In terms of DTDs, this restriction is well captured by the notion of nested relational DTDs (for instance, there is no explicit disjunction). Thus, in the analysis of the remaining two parameters, we will be assuming that the DTDs are nested-relational.

Guessing can also be enforced by the second component of the problem: wildcard and descendant cannot be allowed in the st-tgds if we aim for tractability.

Proposition 4.18   *There exist mappings $\mathcal{M}_1 \in \text{SM}^{nr}(\downarrow, \_, =)$ and $\mathcal{M}_2 \in \text{SM}^{nr}(\downarrow, \downarrow^*, =)$ and queries $Q_1, Q_2 \in \mathbf{CTQ}(\downarrow, =)$, such that both* $\text{CERTAIN}_{\mathcal{M}_1}(Q_1)$ *and* $\text{CERTAIN}_{\mathcal{M}_2}(Q_2)$ *are coNP-complete.*

Proof. The coNP upper bounds follows from Proposition 4.17. Below we prove the lower bound for the first claim. The proof for the second claim can be obtained by replacing _ with $\downarrow^*$.

The reduction is very similar to the one used in the second example, only the selection of literals for each clause is done by permuting the data values in the L_i-children: we choose the literal encoded by the data value stored in L_1.

Thus, the source DTD D_s remains the same, the target DTD D_t is equal to D_s, the st-tgds Σ_{st} are

$$r/C[L_1(x), L_2(y), L_3(z)] \rightarrow r/C[\_(x), \_(y), \_(z)],$$
$$r/V(x, y) \rightarrow r/V(x, y).$$

and the query is $\exists x \exists y\, r\big[V(x, y), C/L_1(x), C/L_1(y)\big]$.   □

In the next section, we will see that the sibling ordering and inequality in st-tgds does not cause trouble. Now, let us move to the analysis of the query language.

One lesson learned from the relational case is that inequality in the query language leads to coNP-hardness. Since the usual translation from the relational setting to the XML setting produces mappings from $\mathrm{SM}^{nr}(\downarrow, =)$, we have the following result.

Corollary 4.19   *There exist a schema mapping $\mathcal{M} \in \mathrm{SM}^{nr}(\downarrow, =)$ and a query Q in $\mathbf{CTQ}\,(\downarrow, =, \neq)$ such that* $\mathrm{CERTAIN}_{\mathcal{M}}(Q)$ *is coNP-complete.*

Similarly, allowing any form of horizontal navigation in queries leads to intractability even for the simplest mappings.

Proposition 4.20   *There exist a schema mapping $\mathcal{M}$ from $\mathrm{SM}^{nr}(\downarrow)$, and two queries $Q_1 \in \mathbf{CTQ}\,(\downarrow, \rightarrow, =), Q_2 \in \mathbf{CTQ}\,(\downarrow, \rightarrow^*, =)$, such that both $\mathrm{CERTAIN}_{\mathcal{M}}(Q_1)$ and $\mathrm{CERTAIN}_{\mathcal{M}}(Q_2)$ are coNP-complete.*

Proof. The proof is almost identical as for Proposition 4.18. The mapping uses the same D_s. The target DTD D_t is

$$
\begin{array}{ll}
r \rightarrow C^* V^* & \qquad V: @a_1, @a_2 \\
C \rightarrow L^* & \qquad L: @b
\end{array}
$$

and the st-tgds Σ_{st} are

$$r/C[L_1(x), L_2(y), L_3(z)] \rightarrow r/C[L(x), L(y), L(z)],$$
$$r/V(x, y) \rightarrow r/V(x, y).$$

Intuitively, we choose the literal having more than two following siblings. Since each C node has at least three L children, clearly at least one literal is chosen for each clause. The query Q_1 is just $\exists x \exists y\, r\big[L(x, y), C[L(x) \rightarrow L \rightarrow L], C[L(y) \rightarrow L \rightarrow L]\big]$. Replacing $\rightarrow$ with $\rightarrow^*$ gives Q_2.   □

We have seen that if we stick to child-based mappings, we cannot extend the query language. But perhaps we can find a more suitable class of mappings? Observe that the mapping in the proof above is very imprecise: the queries use horizontal navigation, and yet the mapping does not specify it at all. It might seem a good idea to demand more precision, for instance, by allowing only $a[b \rightarrow c]$ or $a[c \rightarrow b]$, but not $a[b, c]$. Unfortunately, the reduction above can be modified to obtain hardness for such mappings too. Sibling order in queries inevitably leads to intractability.

In summary, if certain answers are to be tractable, the DTDs should be simple enough, mappings should not use descendent nor wildcard, and queries should not use horizontal navigation nor inequality.

What sense does it make to use sibling order in the mapping if we cannot ask queries about it? Our running example shows how one can meaningfully use sibling order on the source side and store the result on the target side as labeled tuples. In fact, the semantics of the mappings makes it impossible to copy from the source to the target ordered sequences of children of arbitrary length. Hence, whatever we encode on the target side with sibling order, we can equally well encode using labeled tuples, provided we have a little influence on the target DTD. Thus, forbidding horizontal navigation in the target database and queries, we do not lose much in terms of expressiveness.

4.4.3   TRACTABLE QUERY ANSWERING

In this section, we show a polynomial time algorithm for computing certain answers for mappings from $\mathrm{SM}^{\mathrm{nr}}(\downarrow, =)$ and queries from $\mathbf{UCTQ}\,(\downarrow, \downarrow^*, \_, =)$. The methods we develop can be extended to $\mathrm{SM}^{\mathrm{nr}}(\downarrow, \rightarrow, \rightarrow^*, =, \neq)$. To simplify notation, we also assume that each leaf has a single attribute, and internal nodes have no attributes. Removing this assumption poses no difficulties.

The approach, just like in the relational case, is via universal solutions. Recall that U is a universal solution for S under $\mathcal{M}$ if it is a solution for S, and for each other solution T, there is a homomorphism from U to T preserving data values used in S. The following lemma carries over from the relational case.

Lemma 4.21   *If U is a universal solution for a source tree S under a mapping $\mathcal{M}$, and Q is a query in* $\mathbf{UCTQ}\,(\downarrow, \downarrow^*, \rightarrow, \rightarrow^*, \_, =)$, *then for every tuple $\bar{a}$*

$$\bar{a} \in certain_{\mathcal{M}}(Q, S) \iff \bar{a} \in Q(U).$$

Fix a tree S and a mapping $\mathcal{M} = (D_s, D_t, \Sigma_{st})$. Consider the following set of partially valuated tree patterns

$$\Delta_{S,\mathcal{M}} = \{\psi(\bar{a}, \bar{z}) \mid \varphi(\bar{x}, \bar{y}) \rightarrow \exists \bar{z}\, \psi(\bar{x}, \bar{z}) \in \Sigma_{st}, \text{ and } S \models \varphi(\bar{a}, \bar{b})\}.$$

Rename variables in $\Delta_{S,\mathcal{M}}$ so that every pattern uses disjoint sets of variables. Let $\delta_{S,\mathcal{M}}(\bar{z})$ be the pattern obtained by merging at the root all patterns from the modified $\Delta_{S,\mathcal{M}}$. A straightforward check gives the following property.

Lemma 4.22 $T \in \mathrm{SOL}_{\mathcal{M}}(S) \iff T \models D_t$ *and* $T \models \exists \bar{z}\, \delta_{S,\mathcal{M}}(\bar{z})$.

In light of this simple observation, constructing a universal solution for S under $\mathcal{M} \in \mathrm{SM}^{\mathrm{nr}}(\downarrow$, $=$) amounts to finding a "universal" tree satisfying a child-based pattern π (with equalities) and conforming to a nested relational DTD D. To this end, we construct a pattern π' such that

- for every T, if $T \models D$ then $T \models \pi$ iff $T \models \pi'$,

- π' viewed as a tree conforms to D.

We construct this pattern by means of two operations, called *completion* and *merging*.

The aim of the *completion* is to extend tree patterns with all the nodes required by the DTD. As the given pattern uses only $\downarrow$, and DTDs are nested relational, this can be done in a unique way.

For a DTD D, and a tree pattern φ, construct $\mathrm{cpl}_D(\varphi)$ inductively as follows: if σ is a leaf, let

$$\mathrm{cpl}_D(\sigma) = \sigma(y),$$

where y is a fresh variable; if σ is not a leaf, let

$$\mathrm{cpl}_D(\sigma[\psi_1, \ldots, \psi_k]) = \sigma[\mathrm{cpl}_D(\psi_1), \ldots, \mathrm{cpl}_D(\psi_k), \mathrm{cpl}_D(\tau_1), \ldots, \mathrm{cpl}_D(\tau_m)],$$

where $\tau_1, \ldots, \tau_m$ are all the letters τ such that $\sigma \to \ldots \tau \ldots$ or $\sigma \to \ldots \tau^+ \ldots$, and no formula of the form $\tau[\lambda]$ occurs among ψ_i. Note that different occurrences of σ are be completed with different variables.

It is fairly easy to see that the completed formula is equivalent to the original one.

Lemma 4.23   *Let D be a nested relational DTD, and let φ be a tree pattern. For each $T \models D$ and each $\bar{a}$*

$$T \models \varphi(\bar{a}) \quad \textit{iff} \quad T \models \mathrm{cpl}_D\varphi(\bar{a}, \bar{c}) \textit{ for some } \bar{c}.$$

The second operation is called *merging*. For a given φ, it produces an equivalent formula φ' that admits injective homomorphisms in trees conforming to the given DTD. Merging nodes introduces equality constraints on data values, and so the result of the procedure will be a single tree pattern together with a conjunction of equalities. For a given nested relational DTD D and a tree pattern φ, we will construct $\mathrm{mrg}_D(\varphi)$ inductively, adding new equalities to the global set E along the way. If at some point we arrive at an inconsistency between φ and D, we output an unsatisfiable pattern $\perp$. In the beginning the set E is empty. To obtain $\mathrm{mrg}_D(\sigma[\psi_1, \ldots, \psi_k])$ proceed as follows.

1. For each τ such that $\sigma \to \ldots \tau \ldots$ or $\sigma \to \ldots \tau? \ldots$, merge all the ψ_i's starting with τ, i.e.,

   (a) if τ is a leaf, remove from the sequence $\psi_1, \ldots, \psi_k$ all the formulae starting with τ, say $\tau(t_1), \ldots, \tau(t_m)$, save from one, say $\tau(t_1)$, and add equalities $t_1 = t_2, \ldots, t_1 = t_k$ to E,

   (b) if τ is not a leaf, remove from the sequence $\psi_1, \ldots, \psi_k$ all the formulae starting with τ, say $\tau[\bar{\eta}_1], \ldots, \tau[\bar{\eta}_m]$, and add a formula $\mathrm{mrg}_D(\tau[\bar{\eta}_1, \ldots, \bar{\eta}_m])$.

2. Replace all the remaining subformulae ψ_i with $\mathrm{mrg}_D(\psi_i)$.

3. Return $\perp$ if either of the following holds

    (a) some ψ_i is of the form $\rho[\bar{\eta}]$ with ρ not present in the production for σ,

    (b) E contains an equality between two different constants,

    (c) one of the recursive calls returned $\perp$.

4. Return the obtained tree pattern and the equalities from E.

Keep in mind that every recursive call to mrg adds equalities to E.

For a pattern with equalities π, θ, let $\mathrm{mrg}_D(\pi, \theta) = \pi', E \wedge \theta$, where $\mathrm{mrg}_D(\pi) = \pi', E$. Again, proving that the new formula satisfies the required properties is straightforward.

Lemma 4.24   *Let D be a nested relational DTD, and let φ be a tree pattern (with equalities).*

1. For each $T \models D$ and for all $\bar{a}$

$$T \models \varphi(\bar{a}) \quad \textit{iff} \quad T \models \mathrm{mrg}_D\varphi(\bar{a}).$$

2. If φ is satisfiable wrt D, $\mathrm{mrg}_D(\varphi)$ admits injective homomorphisms in trees conforming to D.

The property we postulated follows.

Lemma 4.25   *Let φ be a pattern (with equalities) satisfiable wrt a nested-relational DTD D.*

• *For every $T \models D$ and every $\bar{a}$*

$$T \models \varphi(\bar{a}) \quad \textit{iff} \quad T \models \mathrm{mrg}_D(\mathrm{cpl}_D\varphi)(\bar{a}, \bar{c}) \textit{ for some } \bar{c}.$$

• $\mathrm{mrg}_D(\mathrm{cpl}_D\varphi)$ *viewed as a tree conforms to D*

Let us now return to the construction of a universal solution. Recall the pattern $\delta_{S,\mathcal{M}}$, combining all right hands of st-tgds. Define $\eta_{S,\mathcal{M}} = \mathrm{mrg}_{D_t}(\mathrm{cpl}_{D_t}\delta_{T,\mathcal{M}})$. Without loss of generality, we can assume that $\eta_{S,\mathcal{M}}$ is a pure tree pattern. Indeed, if an equality says that $v = t$, replace each occurrence of v with t, and remove this equality.

Lemma 4.26   *For a every mapping $\mathcal{M}$ from $\mathrm{SM}^{nr}(\downarrow, =)$ and source tree S, the pattern $\eta_{S,\mathcal{M}}$ viewed as a tree is a universal solution.*

Proof. Let U be $\eta_{S,\mathcal{M}}$ viewed as a tree, with variables interpreted as new data values (nulls). Obviously, $U \models \exists \bar{z}\, \eta(\bar{z})$. By Lemma 4.25, $U \models \exists \bar{u}\, \delta_{S,\mathcal{M}}(\bar{u})$ and $U \models D_s$. Using Lemma 4.22, we conclude that U is a solution.

To show that it is universal, take some solution T. By Lemma 4.25, $T \models \exists \bar{z}\, \eta_{S,\mathcal{M}}(\bar{z})$, and so there exists a homomorphism from $\eta_{S,\mathcal{M}}$ to T. As U and $\eta_{S,\mathcal{M}}$ are isomorphic, this gives a homomorphism from U to T, and proves universality of U. $\qquad\square$

From Lemma 4.21 and Proposition 4.26, we immediately get the promised tractability result.

Corollary 4.27 *For every $\mathcal{M} \in \mathrm{SM}^{nr}(\downarrow, =)$ and $Q \in \mathbf{UCTQ}\,(\downarrow, \downarrow^*, \_, =)$, $\mathrm{CERTAIN}_{\mathcal{M}}(Q)$ is computable in polynomial time.*

4.5   SUMMARY

- In XML schema mappings, analogs of st-tgds state how patterns over the source translate into patterns over the targets.

- Conditions imposed by XML schemas on the structure of target instances can contradict conditions imposed by st-tgds. This makes consistency of XML schema mappings an issue even without target dependencies.

- The consistency problem is undecidable in general; in fact, the key feature that leads to undecidability is the ability to impose (in)equality of data values by the mappings. Without this ability, the consistency problem is solvable in exponential time (which is reasonable for problems at the level of schema mappings, not data), and there are useful tractable cases.

- Query answering, even for XML analogs of relational conjunctive queries, can be intractable (coNP-complete, to be exact), and is tractable only under the following restrictions:

    1. mappings that use nested-relational DTDs and patterns with child navigation and equality comparisons only; and

    2. queries that use downward navigation (child, descendant), wildcard, and equality comparisons.

- In this restricted case there is a polynomial-time algorithm that builds a universal solution for a given tree. Then certain answers can be computed by evaluating the query in that solution.

4.6   BIBLIOGRAPHIC COMMENTS

Tree patterns as they are presented here were introduced by Arenas and Libkin [2008], and further extended with horizontal axes and data comparison by Amano et al. [2009]. The patterns were introduced originally to represent conjunctive queries [Björklund et al., 2007, 2008; Gottlob et al., 2004]. It should be noted, however, that to have the full expressive power of conjunctive queries, one should allow DAG patterns, as it is done by Björklund et al. [2008]. David [2008] considers a different kind of semantics based on injective homomorphisms. Expressing injective patterns as CQs requires inequality on node variables. Satisfiability and evaluation of tree patterns is essentially folklore as it appeared in many incarnations in the literature on tree patterns and XPath satisfiability [Amer-Yahia et al., 2002; Benedikt et al., 2005; Björklund et al., 2008; Hidders, 2003]). The presented proof is by Amano et al. [2009].

Systematic investigation into XML data exchange was initiated by Arenas and Libkin [2008], who considered mappings based on restricted patterns disallowing horizontal navigation and data comparisons. Those features were added by Amano et al. [2009]. Nested relational DTDs are considered by Abiteboul et al. [2006]; Arenas and Libkin [2004, 2008]. Empirical studies on their usage are reported by Bex et al. [2004].

Query answering problem for child-based XML mappings was already considered by Arenas and Libkin [2008], who gave a detailed complexity analysis. The influence of sibling order and data comparisons was studied by Amano et al. [2010].

For basic information on tree automata, their decision problems and their complexity, see the survey by Comon et al. [2007].

Bibliography

S. Abiteboul, L. Segoufin, and V. Vianu. Representing and querying XML with incomplete information. *ACM Trans. Database Syst.*, 31(1):208–254, 2006. DOI: 10.1145/1132863.1132869 95

F. Afrati and P. G. Kolaitis. Answering aggregate queries in data exchange. In *Proc. 27th ACM SIGACT-SIGMOD-SIGART Symp. on Principles of Database Systems*, pages 129–138, 2008. DOI: 10.1145/1376916.1376936 36

S. Amano, L. Libkin, and F. Murlak. XML schema mappings. In *Proc. 28th ACM SIGACT-SIGMOD-SIGART Symp. on Principles of Database Systems*, pages 33–42, 2009. 10, 95

S. Amano, C. David, L. Libkin, and F. Murlak. On the tradeoff between mapping and querying power in XML data exchange. In *Proc. 13th Int. Conf. on Database Theory*, pages 155–164, 2010. DOI: 10.1145/1804669.1804689 95

S. Amer-Yahia, S. Cho, L. Lakshmanan, and D. Srivastava. Tree pattern query minimization. *VLDB J.*, 11:315–331, 2002. DOI: 10.1007/s00778-002-0076-7 95

M. Arenas and L. Libkin. A normal form for XML documents. *ACM Trans. Database Syst.*, 29(1): 195–232, 2004. DOI: 10.1145/974750.974757 95

M. Arenas and L. Libkin. XML data exchange: Consistency and query answering. *J. ACM*, 55(2), 2008. DOI: 10.1145/1346330.1346332 10, 95

M. Arenas, P. Barceló, R. Fagin, and L. Libkin. Locally consistent transformations and query answering in data exchange. In *Proc. 23rd ACM SIGACT-SIGMOD-SIGART Symp. on Principles of Database Systems*, pages 229–240, 2004. DOI: 10.1145/1055558.1055592 36

M. Arenas, P. Barceló, and J. L. Reutter. Query languages for data exchange: beyond unions of conjunctive queries. In *Proc. 12th Int. Conf. on Database Theory*, pages 73–83, 2009a. DOI: 10.1007/s00224-010-9259-6 36

M. Arenas, J. Pérez, J. L. Reutter, and C. Riveros. Composition and inversion of schema mappings. *ACM SIGMOD Rec.*, 38(3):17–28, 2009b. DOI: 10.1145/1815933.1815938 64

M. Arenas, J. Pérez, J. L. Reutter, and C. Riveros. Inverting schema mappings: Bridging the gap between theory and practice. *Proceedings of the VLDB Endowment*, 2(1):1018–1029, 2009c. 65

M. Arenas, J. Pérez, and C. Riveros. The recovery of a schema mapping: Bringing exchanged data back. *ACM Trans. Database Syst.*, 34(4):22:1–22:48, 2009d. DOI: 10.1145/1620585.1620589 64, 65

M. Arenas, R. Fagin, and A. Nash. Composition with target constraints. In *Proc. 13th Int. Conf. on Database Theory*, pages 129–142, 2010. DOI: 10.1145/1804669.1804687 64

P. Barceló. Logical foundations of relational data exchange. *ACM SIGMOD Rec.*, 38(1):49–58, 2009. DOI: 10.1145/1558334.1558341 10

M. Benedikt, W. Fan, and F. Geerts. XPath satisfiability in the presence of DTDs. In *Proc. 24th ACM SIGACT-SIGMOD-SIGART Symp. on Principles of Database Systems*, pages 25–36, 2005. DOI: 10.1145/1065167.1065172 95

P. A. Bernstein. Applying model management to classical meta-data problems. In *Proc. 1st Biennial Conf. on Innovative Data Systems Research*, pages 209–220, 2003. 10, 64

P. A. Bernstein and S. Melnik. Model management 2.0: manipulating richer mappings. In *Proc. ACM SIGMOD Int. Conf. on Management of Data*, pages 1–12, 2007. 10

P. A. Bernstein, T. J. Green, S. Melnik, and A. Nash. Implementing mapping composition. *VLDB J.*, 17(2):333–353, 2008. DOI: 10.1007/s00778-007-0059-9 64

G. J. Bex, F. Neven, and J. Van den Bussche. DTDs versus XML Schema: a practical study. In *Proc. 7th Int. Workshop on the World Wide Web and Databases*, pages 79–84, 2004. 95

H. Björklund, W. Martens, and T. Schwentick. Conjunctive query containment over trees. In *Proc. 11th Int. Workshop on Database Programming Languages*, pages 66–80, 2007. DOI: 10.1007/978-3-540-75987-4_5 95

H. Björklund, W. Martens, and T. Schwentick. Optimizing conjunctive queries over trees using schema information. In *Proc. 33rd International Symposium on Mathematical Foundations of Computer Science*, pages 132–143, 2008. DOI: 10.1007/978-3-540-85238-4_10 95

H. Comon, M. Dauchet, R. Gilleron, C. Löding, F. Jacquemard, D. Lugiez, S. Tison, and M. Tommasi. Tree Automata Techniques and Applications, 2007. URL http://tata.gforge.inria.fr/. Accessed on Aug 17th, 2010. 95

C. David. Complexity of data tree patterns over XML documents. In *Proc. 33rd International Symposium on Mathematical Foundations of Computer Science*, pages 278–289, 2008. DOI: 10.1007/978-3-540-85238-4_22 95

A. Deutsch and V. Tannen. Reformulation of XML queries and constraints. In *Proc. 9th Int. Conf. on Database Theory*, pages 225–241, 2003. DOI: 10.1007/3-540-36285-1_15 36

A. Deutsch, A. Nash, and J. B. Remmel. The chase revisited. In *Proc. 27th ACM SIGACT-SIGMOD-SIGART Symp. on Principles of Database Systems*, pages 149–158, 2008. DOI: 10.1145/1376916.1376938 36

R. Fagin. Inverting schema mappings. *ACM Trans. Database Syst.*, 32(4), 2007. DOI: 10.1145/1292609.1292615 64

R. Fagin and A. Nash. The structure of inverses in schema mappings. *To appear in J. ACM*, 2010. 64

R. Fagin, P. G. Kolaitis, R. J. Miller, and L. Popa. Data exchange: semantics and query answering. *Theor. Comp. Sci.*, 336:89–124, 2005a. DOI: 10.1016/j.tcs.2004.10.033 10, 35, 36

R. Fagin, P. G. Kolaitis, and L. Popa. Data exchange: getting to the core. *ACM Trans. Database Syst.*, 30(1):174–210, 2005b. DOI: 10.1145/1061318.1061323 36

R. Fagin, P. G. Kolaitis, L. Popa, and W.-C. Tan. Composing schema mappings: Second-order dependencies to the rescue. *ACM Trans. Database Syst.*, 30(4):994–1055, 2005c. DOI: 10.1145/1114244.1114249 64

R. Fagin, P. G. Kolaitis, L. Popa, and W.-C. Tan. Quasi-inverses of schema mappings. *ACM Trans. Database Syst.*, 33(2):11:1–11:52, 2008. DOI: 10.1145/1366102.1366108 64, 65

R. Fagin, L. M. Haas, M. A. Hernandez, R. J. Miller, L. Popa, and Y. Velegrakis. Clio: Schema mapping creation and data exchange. In A.T. Borgida, V.K. Chaudhri, P. Giorgini, and E.S. Yu, editors, *Conceptual Modeling: Foundations and Applications, Essays in Honor of John Mylopoulos*, pages 198–236. Springer, 2009. DOI: 10.1007/978-3-642-02463-4 10

A. Fuxman, P. G. Kolaitis, R. J. Miller, and W.-C. Tan. Peer data exchange. *ACM Trans. Database Syst.*, 31(4):1454–1498, 2006. DOI: 10.1145/1189769.1189778 36

G. De Giacomo, D. Lembo, M. Lenzerini, and R. Rosati. On reconciling data exchange, data integration, and peer data management. In *Proc. 26th ACM SIGACT-SIGMOD-SIGART Symp. on Principles of Database Systems*, pages 133–142, 2007. 10

G. Gottlob and A. Nash. Efficient core computation in data exchange. *J. ACM*, 55(2), 2008. DOI: 10.1145/1346330.1346334 36

G. Gottlob, C. Koch, and K. U. Schulz. Conjunctive queries over trees. In *Proc. 23rd ACM SIGACT-SIGMOD-SIGART Symp. on Principles of Database Systems*, pages 189–200, 2004. 95

L. Haas. Beauty and the Beast: the theory and practice of information integration. In *Proc. 11th Int. Conf. on Database Theory*, pages 28–43, 2007. DOI: 10.1145/1055558.1055585 10

P. Hell and J. Nešetřil. *Graphs and Homomorphisms*. Oxford University Press, 2004. DOI: 10.1093/acprof:oso/9780198528173.001.0001 36

A. Hernich and N. Schweikardt. CWA-solutions for data exchange settings with target dependencies. In *Proc. 26th ACM SIGACT-SIGMOD-SIGART Symp. on Principles of Database Systems*, pages 113–122, 2007. DOI: 10.1145/1265530.1265547 36

J. Hidders. Satisfiability of XPath expressions. In *Proc. 9th Int. Workshop on Database Programming Languages*, pages 21–36, 2003. DOI: 10.1007/978-3-540-24607-7_3 95

B. Housel, R. Taylor, S. Ghosh, and V. Y. Lum. EXPRESS: a data extraction, processing, and restructuring system. *ACM Trans. Database Syst.*, 2(2):134–174, 1977. DOI: 10.1145/320544.320549 10

T. Imielinski and W. Lipski. Incomplete information in relational databases. *J. ACM*, 31(4):761–791, 1984. DOI: 10.1145/1634.1886 36

P. G. Kolaitis. Schema mappings, data exchange, and metadata management. In *Proc. 24th ACM SIGACT-SIGMOD-SIGART Symp. on Principles of Database Systems*, pages 61–75, 2005. DOI: 10.1145/1065167.1065176 10

P. G. Kolaitis, J. Panttaja, and W.-C. Tan. The complexity of data exchange. In *Proc. 25th ACM SIGACT-SIGMOD-SIGART Symp. on Principles of Database Systems*, pages 30–39, 2006. DOI: 10.1145/1142351.1142357 36

M. Lenzerini. Data integration: a theoretical perspective. In *Proc. 21st ACM SIGACT-SIGMOD-SIGART Symp. on Principles of Database Systems*, pages 233–246, 2002. 10

L. Libkin. Data exchange and incomplete information. In *Proc. 25th ACM SIGACT-SIGMOD-SIGART Symp. on Principles of Database Systems*, pages 60–69, 2006. DOI: 10.1145/1142351.1142360 36

L. Libkin and C. Sirangelo. Data exchange and schema mappings in open and closed worlds. In *Proc. 27th ACM SIGACT-SIGMOD-SIGART Symp. on Principles of Database Systems*, pages 139–148, 2008. DOI: 10.1145/1376916.1376937 36, 64

J. Madhavan and A. Y. Halevy. Composing Mappings Among Data Sources. In *Proc. 29th Int. Conf. on Very Large Data Bases*, pages 572–583, 2003. DOI: 10.1016/B978-012722442-8/50057-4 64

B. Marnette. Generalized schema-mappings: from termination to tractability. In *Proc. 28th ACM SIGACT-SIGMOD-SIGART Symp. on Principles of Database Systems*, pages 13–22, 2009. 36

M. Meier, M. Schmidt, and G. Lausen. Stop the chase: short contribution. In *Proc. 3rd Alberto Mendelzon International Workshop on Foundations of Data Management*, 2009. 36

A. Nash, P. A. Bernstein, and S. Melnik. Composition of mappings given by embedded dependencies. *ACM Trans. Database Syst.*, 32(1):4:1–4:51, 2007. DOI: 10.1145/1206049.1206053 64

F. Neven. Automata, logic, and XML. In *Proc. 11th Annual Conference of the European Association for Computer Science Logic*, pages 2–26, 2002. DOI: 10.1007/3-540-45793-3_2 78

B. ten Cate and P. G. Kolaitis. Structural characterizations of schema-mapping languages. In *Proc. 12th Int. Conf. on Database Theory*, pages 63–72, 2009. DOI: 10.1145/1514894.1514903 36

C. Yu and L. Popa. Semantic adaptation of schema mappings when schemas evolve. In *Proc. 31st Int. Conf. on Very Large Data Bases*, pages 1006–1017, 2005. 64